feeding
a
divided
america

New Century
Gardens and Landscapes
of the American Southwest

BAKER MORROW, Series Editor

Whether practical gardening guides, best plant guides, landscape architecture showcases, or blueprints for urban ecology, books in the New Century Gardens and Landscapes of the American Southwest series address the challenges novice gardeners and skilled practitioners alike face with prolonged droughts, limited water supplies, high-altitude climes, and growing urbanization. Books in this series not only provide practical landscaping advice for backyard gardeners, they dive deep into ecology, built environments, agricultural history, and the emerging discipline of urban ecology. The New Century Gardens and Landscapes of the American Southwest series tackles the environmental questions that many communities in the American West confront as we all work to create healthy, dynamic, and inviting outdoor spaces.

Also available in the New Century Gardens and Landscapes of the American Southwest series:

The Gardens of Los Poblanos by Judith Phillips
Water for the People: The Acequia Heritage of New Mexico in a Global Context edited by Enrique R. Lamadrid and José A. Rivera

feeding a divided america

Reflections of a Western Rancher in the Era of Climate Change

Gilles Stockton

University of New Mexico Press
Albuquerque

© 2024 by Gilles Stockton
All rights reserved. Published 2024
Printed in the United States of America

ISBN 978-0-8263-6610-8 (cloth)
ISBN 978-0-8263-6611-5 (ePub)

Library of Congress Cataloging-in-Publication data is on file with the Library of Congress

Founded in 1889, the University of New Mexico sits on the traditional homelands of the Pueblo of Sandia. The original peoples of New Mexico—Pueblo, Navajo, and Apache—since time immemorial have deep connections to the land and have made significant contributions to the broader community statewide. We honor the land itself and those who remain stewards of this land throughout the generations and also acknowledge our committed relationship to Indigenous peoples. We gratefully recognize our history.

Publication of this book was supported in part by Osuna Nursery.

Cover image by Jesse Gardner on Unsplash
Designed by Isaac Morris
Composed in Iowan Old Style

This book is dedicated to the memory of Wilbur H. Wood, who passed away quite suddenly on March 27, 2023. Wilbur was a good friend, a professional journalist, a professor of creative writing, and a gifted author. He encouraged me to improve my writing skills and hone the concepts expressed in this book.

CONTENTS

AUTHOR'S NOTE	*viii*
PREFACE On the Bear Wags Its Tail Creek	*ix*
INTRODUCTION The Dynamic Backdrop to People's Lives	*1*
Once Upon a Time, Old MacDonald Had a Farm	*10*
Normalize from Reality: Musing on the Rural-Urban Political Divide and the Future of Food	*54*
The Complicity of Consumers	*85*
The Not COOL Story of the Farm Policy Debate	*105*
Bridging the Rural-Urban Divide	*130*
ACKNOWLEDGMENTS	*142*
NOTES	*143*
INDEX	*153*

AUTHOR'S NOTE

These essays are the result of frustration at the limitations of letters to the editor and opinion pieces. I have been writing in this shorter form for years, and my thoughts and opinions have been widely published, primarily in the press devoted to the livestock industry.

But I was frustrated that the issues I was struggling to understand were interconnected in ways I could not express within the limitations of one thousand words. Therefore, in 2019, I decided to write the first essay in this series. There was no intention that this essay would lead to another or that as a whole the essays would ever be published. It was simply an exercise to clarify within my own mind how these seemingly disparate issues have a relationship that affects the lives of rural peoples and instructs their political expressions. At the same time, these issues have repercussions for the future production of food and, ultimately, the food security of all Americans.

This is somewhat of an apology to you, the reader, explaining why these essays are not fully coherent and are, in some respects, repetitive. Although the essays were never conceived to form a coherent whole, ultimately, they do—even if they ask questions to which I cannot supply easy answers. My purpose is to provide the readers with a set of facts about the realities of production agriculture within the context of living in rural America. If both rural and urban people have the same set of facts with which to express their concerns, perhaps they can reach common conclusions. If we cannot reach a rural-urban consensus, the future of our food production capacity shall be imperiled, along with our cohesion as a democracy.

PREFACE

On the Bear Wags Its Tail Creek

The Bear Wags Its Tail creek has flowed through my ranch in central Montana for a long time. However, in the 1870s it was renamed for Henry MacDonald, who accompanied a military survey of central Montana. I always wondered who MacDonald was because there are no MacDonalds who number among the early pioneers of the valley. And the name MacDonald Creek (now typically spelled McDonald Creek) is at odds with its sibling streams: Flatwillow, Elk, Blacktail, Box Elder, Yellow Water, Chippewa, and Shurenuff, which all eventually flow into the Musselshell River that, in turn, empties into the Big Muddy (Missouri River). Those are good names.

I stumbled on this information recently, which saddens me because my father, who has passed away, would have been really tickled to know the original name of the creek. He spent his entire life on the banks of the Bear Wags Its Tail creek and never knew so. As a child, he and his friends played, fished, and swam in the creek. As an adult, he cut hay and watched over sheep in the creek's valley. He also painted the changing moods of the creek and the valley through which it flows. For me, if I look out the window, I see MacDonald Creek, and if I look on the walls of my house, I see MacDonald Creek.

My father, Bill Stockton, was a rancher but also an artist, credited with bringing modernist art forms to Montana. Although he was born into the typical hard upbringing, common for the children of his generation in central Montana, his experiences in World War II drew him to art. He met and married my mother in Paris during the last year of the war. They returned to Paris, with me as a toddler, while my father studied art at the Académie de la Grande Chaumièr. Upon our return to Montana, he took over the small ranch from his mother and raised sheep, painting in the winter when outside work was not as demanding.

The cultures who have inhabited this valley over the last thirteen thousand or so years have all stamped their own personalities and requirements on the landscape. Just upstream on my neighbors' land was a long-term habitation site. The neighbors found numerous stone tools and even an obsidian stone from which new arrowheads would have been struck. A few more miles upstream are vibrant cliff paintings depicting warriors carrying large circular shields. There is also a buffalo jump with a trace of the wall that was used to herd the animals to their death. This valley was well populated before horses came to this part of the West, a technological change that forever altered the lives of the peoples inhabiting the area, ultimately resulting in the mounted Plains Indians with whom we are more familiar.[1]

A word first about Henry MacDonald. He worked his way upriver on a steamboat in 1866, just eighteen years old and a wounded veteran of the Civil War. Henry took up with the trappers and woodhawks who had a small settlement where the Musselshell meets the Missouri. These men trapped in the winter and cut wood for the steamboats during the summer. They were the tail end of the mountain man era that started when Captains Meriwether Lewis and William Clark led the Corps of Discovery expedition through the upper Missouri in 1805. Lewis and Clark were followed by the American Fur Company, which brought knives, axes, pots, blankets, beads, whiskey, and guns to trade for furs and buffalo hides. The guns were the game changer, giving a military advantage to the tribes who were the first to acquire sufficient numbers. According to Lewis and Clark, the Sioux (a name that refers to a gathering of Lakota, Dakota, and Nakota tribal bands) who lived along the banks of the middle stretch of the Missouri, were among the first to get guns, which were used to accelerate the interminable intertribal wars.[2]

Gold mining also fits into this story. Gold was first discovered in southwest Montana in 1860, attracting a horde of miners and increasing the steamboat traffic on the Missouri. More steamboats, more need for firewood, more work for MacDonald and his friends.

According to Henry MacDonald's biographer, who was also his daughter, Henry got on well with most of the tribes, particularly the Crow (Apsáalooke).[3] But the Sioux were a different story.

Henry survived numerous battles, skirmishes, and ambushes here in central Montana. The Sioux were raiding and stealing horses from MacDonald, his fellow settlers, and the other tribes living in central Montana. The Sioux's last big win was on the banks of the Little Bighorn River in 1876. That victory pretty much marked the end of the frontier in the Montana Territory.

About the time that Henry MacDonald's name was imposed on the geography, cattle and sheep began to show up, changing the culture and the landscape once again. The buffalo were gone and the grass abundant. The little town just downstream from my ranch is called Grass Range. I speculate that it was named for basin wildrye, a tall bunchgrass that now only survives along the little, undisturbed bends of the creek. Although cowboys, cattle drives, and cattle barons have an outsize place in our western mythology, around here that era actually lasted less than ten years. It all froze in the winter of 1886–1887, when most of the cattle died.

The sheep survived the winter better because they are naturally more insulated from the cold and more adept at digging through the snow to find grass. Bands of sheep were being herded about as homesteaders started to arrive in the late nineteenth century. The water right for this ranch was filed in 1891. My grandparents, though, were relatively late arrivals on the homesteading wave that followed the construction of railroads crossing Montana. My grandmother Julia Erikson worked as a telephone operator in Minneapolis, the high-tech job of that time available to women. In 1910–1911, she and two of her girlfriends took the notion to come to Montana and homestead.

My grandfather William Murray Stockton Sr. came to Montana sometime in the 1890s, and by 1910, he was working as the surveyor for the construction of a railroad spur from Lewistown to Grass Range and on to Winnett. The route for the spur that my grandfather surveyed went right down the middle of the MacDonald Creek Valley. My grandparents met at a point on the rail line called Becket, just three miles upstream from the ranch. But good homestead sites were already in short supply, so they filed on a dry-land allotment south of Winnett in Petroleum County.

My grandmother died in 1975. After she passed, we got an extraordinary communication from a lady in Aberdeen, South Dakota. She had moved into an old house and in the attic she found a box of correspondence, including a bundle from my grandmother to her friend Anna Kittelson. Seeing Grandma as a young newlywed and then as a mother with her first baby was illuminating. However, one aspect of her letters was a bit jarring: she repeatedly urged Anna to come to Montana to claim a homestead—not to be a farmer but to prove up on the land and then sell at a big profit.

We have come to believe a revisionist history of that homestead movement—that it was all a big scam perpetrated by the railroad companies to create a built-in market for themselves.[4] Reputable sources advanced the idea that the "rain would follow the plow." Accordingly, the settling of the Great Plains would change the land from a desert to a fertile oasis of agriculture. And apparently my grandmother was an enthusiastic supporter of settling the Great Plains.

There is, in fact, a big boost to soil fertility when ancient sod is first plowed and seeded to a cash crop. With fertile soil and good rains during the first decades of the homestead era, the farmers brought in bountiful crops. That fertility started to wane around 1920, just when the climate turned to a drier pattern. By then, no one was willing to pay big money for a dry-land homestead. My grandfather died in 1920, leaving my grandmother with three little girls and a baby on the way. In 1923, the homestead shack burned down, and my grandmother moved her four children to the town of Winnett, where she sold milk from a couple of cows and took in washing for the old bachelors.

Above the piano in my living room is a painting of a grim-looking woman with a baby on her lap, surrounded by three unsmiling little girls, an image that my father painted from a family photograph. But Grandma was tenacious. She had a garden at her little shack in Winnett, grazed her milk cows along the barrow ditches and railroad right-of-way, and took in laundry. She sent her two oldest daughters to college and then in 1933–1934 met a man who had just bought a place three miles upstream from Grass Range. But before they could marry, he died, leaving my grandmother the ranch. Paying the back taxes in the middle of the Great Depression was a struggle, but somehow she found the money.

With the addition of the railroad, the homesteaders transformed the MacDonald Creek Valley. There had been a stagecoach stop and post office at Grass Range since 1883, but that was about the size of it. The first train reached Grass Range on August 13, 1913. According to the Grass Range History Committee,

> By the time the first train rolled into town, there were three lumber yards, three or more hotels, and several rooming houses, ten restaurants, many stores, several saloons, a blacksmith shop, and three or more livery stables. There was a Moose Hall with a dance floor and apartments upstairs, and a meat market and the Palace Merc on the first floor. There were two grain elevators, a land office, a drug store, and lawyer's office. At that time, the town was served by two doctors.[5]

Soon came a Methodist church and a two-room school. There were three garages with gas stations that also sold cars and farm machinery. The town had its own newspaper, and in 1922, a high school was built. Back then, there were one-room schools located all up and down the valley, so no child had to walk or ride a horse more than three miles. Each of these schools was the focus for a little community. The high school in Grass Range had a dormitory to accommodate the older kids who came in from a radius of twenty miles around the town.

My father graduated from Grass Range High School in 1938, one of seven in his senior class. However, by then, the whole community was falling apart. People were abandoning their homesteads, along with their dreams of being independent landowners. What had been a growing town turned into a wide main street lined with empty buildings.

By the time I started grade school in 1952, all that was left on Main Street were three gas stations, two stores, two bars, two restaurants, a grain elevator, the train depot, the post office, and a barber shop. The railroad quit running by 1970, and in 1975, the tracks were pulled up and the right-of-way incorporated into the surrounding hayfields.

Today there is only one business left on Main Street—a garage. We still have a post office, but it was downgraded to provide minimal services. Grass Range does have a bar, a grocery store, two restaurants, and two gas stations, but those are located along the highway that now goes around the town.

When I was in high school, in the twelve-mile stretch of the valley between Grass Range and Forest Grove, Montana, there were fifteen working farms and ranches. Now there are only five. The former ranches are now summer and hunting residences for three millionaires, plus two hundred thousand acres owned by two billionaire brothers from Texas. The land still feeds cows belonging to the community's few surviving ranchers, who lease the grass from the absentee landlords—who, in turn, are more interested in raising elk.

The Grass Range High School is still here and is still the heart of the community, but all the one-room schoolhouses are derelicts. I graduated in 1964, with nine other classmates. The class of 2020 had three graduates. Whereas in the past the basketball team from Winnett was the hated rival, now to have enough kids to form the boys' and girls' basketball teams, the two towns cooperate. The Grass Range Rangers play in the black-and-white uniform of the Winnett Rams.

So how do we survive as a community when the local businesses can no longer meet our needs? Modern cars and pickups go much faster than those we had in the 1950s and 1960s, and the highways are much better. When I was young, a family trip to Billings, our big city a hundred miles to our south, was an overnight affair. Now, if you need a part for your haying machinery, it is a quick trip there and back with a stop at Walmart for groceries. We also have a whole new category of residents: the retired. Local retirees live in the old houses and double-wides scattered around the town, and out-of-state retirees have purchased small acreages in the surrounding hills. Without the Social Security checks mailed every month to these retirees, none of the businesses left in town would survive very long.

There are those who maintain that our communities, our way of life, and our form of agriculture is simply not viable. This was certainly the message that Frank and Deborah Popper, professors at Rutgers University in New Jersey, advanced in the late 1980s. According to Anne Matthews, writing in the *New York Times Magazine* in 1990,

> Frank Popper, chairman of the Rutgers urban studies department and an international expert on land-use planning, and his wife, Deborah Epstein Popper, a Rutgers geographer, want to convert much of America's prairie outback into public domain for its original residents—the buffalo. According to their research, vast areas in the 10 Great Plains states—from the 98th meridian to the Rockies—are already experiencing or will undergo a sharp decline in population and prosperity.
>
> In Nebraska, for instance, says Deborah Popper, the distressed locals are found in counties "that have at least a 50 percent population loss since 1930. An over-10-percent loss between 1980 and 1988. Four people or fewer per square mile. High median age. Twenty percent or more in poverty. New annual construction investment under $50 per capita. All very bad news."
>
> Over the next 30 years, the Poppers argue, the depressed areas should become a huge reserve, more than 139,000 square miles of open land and wildlife refuge. That zone, which the Poppers call the Buffalo Commons, includes much of the western Dakotas, western Nebraska and eastern Montana; portions of Kansas, Oklahoma and Texas, and selected counties in Colorado, New Mexico and Wyoming.
>
> Set in place, the Buffalo Commons—most likely to be administered by a consortium of government agencies and private groups—would be the world's largest national park, an act of ecological restoration that would, the Poppers contend, boldly reverse more than 100 years of American

history. Commons visitors would once again see the heart of the continent as Lewis and Clark first knew it, a true frontier of waving grass and migrant game.[6]

The poverty and population loss that the Poppers observed was attributed to inappropriate agricultural production methodologies. Seemingly, the Poppers did not perceive that the poverty of rural America could be the consequence of deliberate rural policy designed to force small farmers and ranchers from the land. Frank Popper may have been an international expert in land use planning and Deborah Popper a geographer, but apparently neither knew much about animal husbandry or range science.

I will make the bold statement, based on decades of personal observation, studying the situation, and working the land, that the ranching system that has evolved on the Great Plains following the collapse of the homestead farming era is the only actual sustainable example of agriculture within the main branches of US food production. *Sustainable agriculture* is a term that is thrown around a lot, without a clear definition, ultimately meaning whatever the writer or speaker wants it to mean. To me, *sustainable agriculture* means a form of production that incrementally improves its land base—and the land devoted to ranching *has* been incrementally enhanced. Eastern Montana grasslands are, overall, better than when Lewis and Clark came up the Missouri in 1805. The biomass that these plains, hills, and ridges now produce exceeds what was here two hundred years earlier, and it does so much more predictably even during periods of drought.

What the survivors of the homestead era learned the hard way is that farming on most of the soils of this dry environment is not sustainable. However, these hills do produce highly nutritious grasses. This transition from farming to ranching was the result of many experiments by thousands of animal husbandmen. What they eventually perfected was a way to raise livestock in a manner that improves the rangeland.

Essentially what the modern ranching system does is reverse the natural pattern of the wildlife. Drinking water is the limiting factor for animals grazing these plains. In the past, permanent sources of water were miles apart, particularly in midsummer and into the fall. This meant that the herds of bison and elk had to congregate in the few creek and river valleys when water was no longer available in the intermittent streams that flow from the hills and ridges. Consequently, the valleys were overused, and the hills and ridges were undergrazed. The early photographs of MacDonald Creek show no trees. Today the course of the stream is well protected with willows, chokecherry, box elders, and cottonwoods.

When Henry MacDonald came up the Missouri in 1866, the first buffalo he saw were floating carcasses. Apparently, the bison had a habit of crossing the river at places where they could not exit on the opposite bank. As a result, numbers of them would drown at the base of the steep banks. This is not inconceivable, as I have witnessed wildebeests doing the same thing crossing the Mara River in southern Kenya. For whatever reason—perhaps they forget that the grass is not greener on the other side—the huge herds constantly swim the river, first one way and then back again the next day. Each time, the crocodiles get a few, but many more drown because they can't climb the steep banks on the far side. It all has to do with the need for water and the animal's reluctance to make the long trek back to where there is grass.

Mother Nature has her systems, but they are, inevitably, wasteful of both the base resource and the life-forms. Nature does not tend toward a permanent equilibrium. Instead, there is a constant fluctuation between abundance and disaster. Agriculture is Homo sapiens' attempt to rationalize and maximize the production of food by modifying what nature would otherwise dictate. In the modern ranching system, dams and wells are strategically constructed in the hills and ridges previously lacking permanent water. By controlling access to water, ranchers also control the grazing, resulting in the entire landscape being rationally utilized.

A cow needs on average 25 pounds of grass (dry-matter basis) per day. The hills and ridges produce, under moderate grazing pressure, 250–500 pounds per acre. However, only half of the grass can be harvested in any one season without causing rangeland deterioration.

Meanwhile, the alfalfa hayfields in the valleys along the creeks produce 2,000 pounds per acre. This means that 1.5 acres of hayfield will produce enough fodder to feed a cow for the 4 months of winter. This is balanced for the other 8 months by 24–48 acres of hill pasture. When managed conservatively, the range condition of those hills improves. In contrast, under natural grazing by wildlife, the rangeland was used in an uneven matter, with the grasslands closest to water overgrazed and the furthest underutilized.

The Poppers got it fundamentally wrong. Our communities in the Rocky Mountain West *are* failing, but not because the forms of agriculture we practice are nonproductive. Instead, we are failing as the result of a national policy that systematically confiscates the food we raise for less than it costs to produce. The effects of this policy are made all the worse by wealthy persons looking for retirement homes and recreation opportunities, who bid up the cost of land beyond what its agricultural productivity can sustain.

INTRODUCTION

The Dynamic Backdrop to People's Lives

*They hang the man and flog the woman
Who steals the goose from off the common
Yet let the greater villain loose
That steals the common from the goose.*

This rhyme dates to the seventeenth century, a time that we can trace as the beginning of industrialized agriculture. Landlords, the aristocracy of Great Britain, saw profit in expelling the peasants with whom they had had centuries of mutual and reciprocal association. Instead, on the dispossessed farmers' fields (the commons), the aristocrats raised sheep to supply the beginnings of the Industrial Revolution. The wool mills got their raw materials, along with their choice of cheap labor.

The rapidly growing demand for food and goods to feed the manufacturing and finance centers of Europe and the New World resulted in an international commerce that enslaved peoples in Africa for labor on sugar, cotton, and tobacco plantations in the Americas. Privation, exploitation, and slavery have been, from the very beginning, the exorbitant price many rural folks have paid for the Industrial Revolution—a price that is integral to how our society is structured and colors everything that we believe about food and how food is produced.

Today the dictates of industrialization in agriculture have almost eliminated the need for farmers (those men and women who get their hands dirty tilling the soil and harvesting the produce). All that is now required in much of the modern agriculture-industrial complex is capital, management, specialized consultation, and labor—few real farmers. And a good part of the labor is rapidly being replaced with automation. According to statistics from the United States Department of Agriculture (USDA) in 2019, 209,007 farms produced 78.7 percent of commodity sales. The other 21.7 percent is shared by 1,820,192 small family farms.[1]

Yet the farmer continues to have a mythological place in our collective national psyche. We have been conditioned to believe that our food is raised in a happy place, by a jovial farmer, his adoring wife, and three wholesome, freckle-faced children, with a contented collie sitting at their feet. This image sells food in the supermarket. The industrialized agricultural system does not want consumers to see or think about the reality: the exploitation of the land, animals, and people that occurs to produce food at the lowest prices in the developed world.

The essays in this book explore the rural-urban divide and how that determines the structure of our society and the landscapes in which we live. *Landscape* is an interesting portmanteau of a word. It refers to a subject of easel painting. It describes gardens and public spaces and is used to contemplate far-flung vistas. Landscape ecology is the science of studying and improving relationships between ecological processes. *Cultural landscape* connotes the context of human relationships within a society—the dynamic backdrop to people's lives—how human relationships, including rural resentments and urban expectations, manifest itself within the political economy of this nation.

On TV when they show peoples' voting preferences, it is striking how rural counties in the United States typically show up as red and urban counties as blue. This divide is as dramatic as they come. I explore the dynamics causing this divide from a rural, agricultural perspective as a third-generation rancher in central Montana. My thoughts have been guided by my personal observances and experiences as a sheep and cattle rancher, augmented by my work in Africa promoting economic development among pastoral peoples. The rural-urban divide is by no means limited to the United States. It is indeed global. Farmers and pastoralists in Africa are somehow frozen in prehistory while simultaneously trying to connect to the global economy. It is a wrenching dichotomy that we, in the industrialized part of the world, tend to ignore, an oversight that is increasingly not working. The troubles in the farthest, poorest places, are now landing on our doorsteps.

Against the Grain

Cities and agriculture have been linked since prehistory, when farming was first practiced in Mesopotamia. Without agriculture, the first cities could not have existed, and, according to James C. Scott, Sterling Professor of Political Science and professor of anthropology at Yale University, in the absence of cities, agriculture was not necessary. In his provocative book *Against the Grain*, Professor Scott argues that the basic principles of agriculture and animal husbandry were understood long before there were any cites where the concentration of people required systematic agriculture.[2]

Neolithic hunter-gatherers (a close friend makes the undoubtedly true point that because women gathered most of the food, this should be stated as "gatherer-hunters") living along the Tigris and Euphrates Rivers had no real need to toil under the sun to till fields and herd animals. It was not until there was a surplus of people that systematic agriculture was needed, which corresponded with the development of the first cites in the land between two rivers.

But those earliest cites were, apparently, authoritarian states that forced people to work the land to supply the needs of a military elite. Naturally, people ran away when they could, necessitating campaigns to capture more workers. Hence, cities, agriculture, and slavery have been interlocked throughout human history.

After millennia of a coercive relationship between cities and farmers, it is no wonder that rural agricultural people look upon "urban elites" as a kind of suspicious, albeit vaguely defined, political tyranny. In these days, the boundary between rural and urban is fluid. Farmers can sell their land and pursue whatever career their talents allow in the urban metropoles. Conversely, urban people can, if they have acquired enough money, buy a farm or ranch to hunt, fish, raise grapes, and train cutting horses. Yet US agricultural policy and the structure of global agricultural markets is made by and designed for the benefit of wealthy elites and an urban population. This is the crux of much of our current political polarization.

Why Does Rural (and Working Class) America Vote for the Republican Party?

Independent farmers and ranchers love their work. If there were an actual profit to be made, farming would be an ideal life. However, alcoholism runs rampant among America's farmers, and suicide rates are high.[3] According to American Addiction Centers, when compared to cities, rural communities have higher rates of alcohol and methamphetamine use, along with rising rates of abuse of other substances.[4] Financial stress and uncertainty under our industrialized agricultural system are what make life on farms and ranches unpleasant, not the work. And the fact of the matter is that this is the result of deliberate policy.

But farmers are not the only ones living in rural America. A class society—as in much of the United States—exists in rural areas, with bankers, other main street businesspeople, and medical and legal professionals at the top of the economic ladder because they typically make the most money and, therefore, presumably enjoy the most political clout. Wealthy farmers and ranchers are part of this elite too, but their work and lifestyle are not necessarily compatible with that experienced by main street and they often do not run in the same social circles.

On a lower rung of the social ladder are the middle class: teachers, government employees, truck drivers, mechanics, carpenters, mom-and-pop-store owners. All part of the many occupations needed to make a functional rural community. However, many of the brightest of rural America's young people have moved to urban centers in search of well-paying jobs and opportunities, leaving behind an underclass in their absence. Those left behind are a growing segment of rural society—and an increasingly unstable one, as they move from town to town chasing the next job or the promise of even cheaper housing, too often poorly educated and sometimes prone to abusing alcohol, meth, and opioids. As a result, both documented and undocumented migrant workers are an increasingly important segment in agriculture.

Most small-to-medium-size farms don't need as much farm labor as in the past. Many of the chores are now being done with expensive machines. Farmers could employ more workers and use smaller, less expensive machinery, but competent help is harder and harder to find. Farmers cannot risk putting a young, inexperienced, incompetent kid on expensive equipment. This dilemma is more and more being met by guest workers from south of the border. Large, industrialized factory farms seemingly prefer migrant workers because they are cheap and reliable. Chicken, hog, and dairy factory farms, along with the slaughter and processing plants, are all dependent on low-paid, sometimes undocumented, migrant labor. These people may not be enslaved, but they are too often economically desperate and easily taken advantage of.

Is it irony or hypocrisy that rural America primarily voted for a president whose main promise was to build a wall to keep out the only people willing to work for very low pay and who are competent enough to do that work?

Guns, God, and Walls

There is a situation that every rancher learns is potentially dangerous. If a cow becomes seriously stressed, if, for instance, she gets herself mired in the mud at a water hole and you have to pull her out, it takes a moment or two for her to get her bearings and on her feet. You need to be very careful removing the ropes from around her neck and legs, because in her mind you are the one who caused her pain and trauma, never mind that you just saved her life.

People instinctively react the same way as the traumatized cow. Many have trouble articulating their pain and anger, particularly those who you might say suffer from what I call political extremist personality disorder (PEPD). I know there is no such diagnosis, but there should be. Although sufferers tend to congregate on the Far Right of the political spectrum, they exist on the Far Left as well, including various iterations of what is often lumped into the modern environmental movement. The key emotion is anger, and it seems to be cultivated as if it is the goal rather than used as a spur to resolve grievances.

It is not really the threat of losing guns and possible restrictions of the Second Amendment that incense rural America but rather a fear of losing their idealized sense of freedom, a way to live free from interference. What defines many in rural America is the ideal of being independent, living a life of responsibility, asking little from anyone, and defending what they have accomplished from those who would take it away.

By the same token, in adopting an uncompromising stance that "life begins at conception," rural America is sending a message that "we" are more moral, compassionate, and godly than those who we perceive to live with no social rules. Never mind that we all depend on others and that living in a community—or a nation—requires compromise and rules in the interest of the common good. What rural Americans are telling the United States is that we are hurting and angry and that you—an unspecified you—are the cause of our pain.

A multicultural, complex, modern society requires tolerance and the acceptance of the behavior of other people and social groups. And when technology has been morphing at light speed, and the world is getting smaller and smaller and smaller, yet more interconnected than ever, it is hard to for people to pivot. The daily news brings images of atrocity into our living rooms. People are blown up right there in front of our eyes over incomprehensible issues. Mobs, dressed in robes and turbans, chant "death to the Great American Satan." We don't understand what is motivating this hatred against us. And perhaps they do not either because of the fear and uncertainty in their lives—someone must be held responsible! But the threat to us is real, not theoretical, even if the probability of being personally harmed is remote.

It is a scary world that technology has brought into our homes and into our lives. Fear is a basic emotion; putting that fear into a realistic perspective requires nonemotional, abstract reasoning, but intellectual response never trumps raw emotion. This is what the media and politicians know so well, and while the rest of us struggle to make sense out of conflicting thoughts and emotions, they manipulate our fears. Couple all that with economic stress in the life you have been trying to put together in your peaceful agricultural, rural community—the natural response is anger.

There is also something that many rural people know in their bones that those on the political Left seemingly dismiss. New people coming into a community, or into a nation, in such drastic numbers that there is a demographic shift—a shift in cultural norms—is not necessarily all for the good. Humans have a genetic inheritance from our primate ancestors that makes us suspicious of others. According to Jared Diamond, gatherer-hunter groups in the jungles of New Guinea tended to kill anyone who was not part of their immediate clan, because they just might be dangerous.[5] It is not pretty, but we human beings are built that way all the same.

Behavior that might preserve clan and tradition in the jungles of New Guinea is no way to run a modern, technologically complex society. But that is an intellectual position, not an emotional one. History is a long story of tribal migrations that, through force of arms and sheer numbers overwhelm, invade, subjugate, and occupy other people's land and communities. A few centuries on a new wave of invaders conquer the original invaders, and the whole cycle is repeated. None of us are ethnically pure, because our ancestors have invaded, and have been invaded, numerous times. Usually, the results were not pleasant for the losing side.

The last mass tribal migration in North America were Europeans who conquered and appropriated the land of the Native Americans. Most Americans of European ancestry are proud of the nation our ancestors have built, albeit on stolen land, and there is much reason for that pride. But our ancestors also committed atrocities against Native peoples and African Americans, for which we should hold no pride. The United States is facing a demographic shift as the numbers and political influence of Native Americans, African Americans, Latinos, and Asian Americans increase. Fearful of becoming culturally irrelevant, many in the white community of rural America suspect—rightly or wrongly—that they will not be treated any better than they have historically treated people of color.

A wall on the border between the United States and Mexico is a pathetic idea. Of course, it will not stop the tide of economic migrants and asylum seekers. For people to stay where they were born and raised, they need peace, justice, and opportunity. The reality is that we live in a complex multiethnic, multicultural, global technological age, and we must find the means to be mutually tolerant. The alternatives—fascism, a police state, theocracy—are unacceptable.

Why the Rural Anger

As a farmer, if you follow the advice of all the experts—the US secretary of agriculture to purchase more land, the banker to borrow more money, and the county agent on what to plant and how—and if you work hard and bring in bountiful crops and yet still fail, this is cause for anger. The foodstuffs you produce are needed by every person three times each day. Consumers obviously want and appreciate what you sell, but because of low margins, you fail. The town where you do your shopping, where you went to school, and where you attend church is half the size as when you were young—this is cause for anxiety and anger.

Your children live a thousand miles away and have good jobs, but one child wants desperately to take over the ranch, and you shake your head and explain that it is just not possible. Costs of production are too high, returns too low, and land prices too exorbitant to justify ranching or farming as an enterprise. The ranch next door, along with three adjoining ranches, has been bought by an urban billionaire. This land is where you used to camp when you were a teenager, hunted for mule deer, and rode to help the neighbors gather cattle. Now it is off limits. When the time comes and they put you out on asphalt pasture, your only option will be to sell to that billionaire neighbor, whom you have never met. This is all cause for anger.

Rural America has been in a slow decline for the last few decades. Farmers and ranchers were promised that if we bought and leased more land and got a bigger tractor that we would be "efficient." We would have an "economy of scale." After all, the experts said, countries in Asia need your wheat and love the beef you raise. But the goalpost has been moved again and again, and you never reach the promised point of "efficiency" or "economy of scale." "Oh," they will tell you, "it is the market! Supply and demand! There is too much wheat and there are too many cows. China did not import as much as was expected." Yet the wheat mills are doing fine, the beef-packer is making money, the price for bread and beef in the supermarket is up. Everyone is making a profit except the farmer and rancher, who go hat in hand to the banker asking for an extension on their operating loan. Next year will be better. It is always next year.

Farmers and ranchers are a minority even in their rural communities, but their concerns dominate the politics of rural America. Through the following essays, I explore how the structure of agricultural markets have been co-opted and distorted to meet the dictates of international corporations, not American farmers and ranchers. This essay was originally written in the spring 2020, at the beginning of the COVID-19 pandemic, when suddenly our global food production and distribution systems began to show serious cracks. Industrialized, vertically integrated agriculture is dependent on a cheap, easily exploitable workforce, and when those workers became sick, entire segments of the food supply chain lurched to a halt. COVID-19 is now with us forever, and most of us survived the initial shock. But what other threats to our lives and economy are we to face? When we do, we will again experience food shortages and price spikes, made all the worse because America has way too few real farmers and way too many predatory corporations.

Once Upon a Time, Old MacDonald Had a Farm

Behind the tractor rolled the shining disks, cutting the earth with blades—not plowing but surgery. . . . The driver sat in his iron seat and he was proud of the straight lines he did not will, proud of the tractor he did not own or love, proud of the power he could not control. And when that crop grew, and was harvested, no man had crumbled a hot clod in his fingers and let the earth sift past his fingertips. No man had touched the seed, or lusted for the growth. Men ate what they had not raised, had no connection with the bread. The land bore under iron, and under iron gradually died; for it was not loved or hated, it had no prayers or curses.
—John Steinbeck, *The Grapes of Wrath*, 1939

The past, present, and future for writer John Steinbeck's fictional Joad family was bleak. Drought and the Great Depression dispossessed them of their lives as farmers in Oklahoma. Their present, in California, was marginal and unstable. Too many economic migrants, not enough work. Their potential resurrection as farmers was doubtful, because industrialization and mechanization in agriculture was making that role superfluous and outside of their financial means.

Respect was lacking for the Joads and the hundreds of thousands of real families in their dilemma. Respect is what has been stripped from the cultivation of food and, by extension, from the food itself. The preparation and consumption of food is central to human activities—the daily ritual of communally breaking bread. The seasonal celebrations of religion and tradition are ultimately centered on the preparation and consumption of food.

But the food itself—now almost all supplied by global, interconnected industries—receives no respect. Purchasing food at a supermarket results in little joy. The shelves at the superstores are overflowing. The presentation of what is being offered is attractive, professionally designed to be so, but I, at least, find little joy in the action of purchasing food in a supermarket.

Contrast that to the experience at a farmers' market or an open-air market in any part of the world. Or consider the excursion to buy food from the neighborhood shops in Paris or one of the ethnic neighborhoods in New York. Bread from the bakery, meat from the butcher, vegetables and fruit from the greengrocer, and cheese from the deli. This shopping mission may be a daily chore, but it is a human and *humane* chore. It is a transaction between people who know each other and respect what is being sold and purchased.

Agricultural industrialization has stripped respect from the land. The animals who live their brief lives in a factory farm and give those lives to the mountain of food receive no respect. The industrial system of food production is efficient, if one disregards the externalities, and results in food so cheap that there is no need to conserve. Food that is the least blemished is garbage.

Respect is also denied to the people who live on the land. Today's surviving farmers, like the fictional Joads, are being dispossessed of their farms but in little, incremental steps that drain what equity they have accrued. Eventually they sell, usually to a larger neighbor. Inevitably, that neighbor sells to an even larger farmer or an out-of-state multimillionaire. In the process, rural America is hollowed out, deprived of its purpose.

Many people probably think they know all about farming. After all, what is there to know? Any idiot can do it, as it is the realm of peasants, villains, churls, serfs, and slaves. A century ago, just about everyone was still connected to the production and marketing of food in one way or another, so farming fits within the parameters of societal expectations as something any fool can do.

So who are the farmers? What do they raise? How are agricultural markets structured? What are the underlying economic realities? We must answer these questions to have a common framework. Only then can we ask the question of whether farming, as it has evolved in today's America, meets our national needs and whether it will meet the needs of the future.

The Dispiriting Economics of Farming

If we are to have a discussion about the structure of agriculture in the United States, as well as its underlying consequences, we need to first wade through some statistics. Only then can we have a common framework within which to debate.

The USDA publishes detailed statistics, but it takes a certain amount of work to make any sense of them. According to the 2019 *Agricultural Statistics Annual*, as of 2018, there were 2,029,200 farm entities in the country, with an average farm size of 443 acres. The total acreage under production was 899,500,000.[1]

That is hard to grasp. Perhaps easier to grasp is that agricultural land comprises of 1,405,468 square miles, an area roughly 1,200 by 1,200 miles. Since the land area of the contiguous United States is 2,954,841 square miles, agriculture occupies almost half of the total land area—even more than half if you count the grazing lands leased from the Bureau of Land Management (BLM) and the USDA Forest Service.

By contrast, the land base in urban areas amounts to 114,840 square miles and is increasing at the rate of 781 square miles per year. This would be a square with 340 miles on a side, with an area of 28 miles by 28 miles added to it each year. They aren't making any more land and it does not disappear, but farmland does get paved over. There may come a time when we will regret how negligent urban areas have been in their consumption of prime farmland.

According to the USDA, within a population of 332 million people, 2 million farms own and/or control half of the land area in the United States. Most farms are classified as family farms, so, presumably, many are owned and operated by a spousal team. You would think that Americans who identify with the modern environmental movement would respect the cumulative knowledge of farmers and ranchers that comes from owning the land, living with the land, and working the land. After all, farmers own a significant portion of "the environment" and have intimate knowledge of the land they steward. But strangely, many do not seem to value that expertise. A war has now developed between production agriculture and the people concerned with watersheds, soils, wildlife, and outdoor recreation. This animosity plays a major factor in the political dysfunction currently paralyzing America. It fuels an already raging rural-urban cultural divide.

When we drill down into the number of farms—the reality of who owns much of the land in the United States—the food production system becomes more and more skewed. The USDA categorizes farmland ownership among five broad income ranges. The first is gross farm income of up to $10,000. Out of the total 2,029,200 farms, half (1,034,892, or 51 percent) fit in this category and essentially do not factor in the total US food production.

Add together the next two categories—farms that annually sell between $10,000 and $350,000 of production—and you get another 785,300 farms for a grand total of 1,820,192 "small family farms." However, these three categories together account for only 21.3 percent of the total production of food in the United States. This leaves just 209,007 agricultural production units producing 78.7 percent of the crops.

The USDA classifies 166,394 of the larger farms as "family farms," even though many of these are family corporations in which some of the owners may have little connection to the land. For them, it may be just an investment inherited from a grandparent. Therefore, the definition of a family farm becomes very blurry. The remaining 42,613 agricultural entities are owned by agricultural corporations not considered to be family farms. The 42,613 corporate farms plus 36,526 of the very largest family farm corporations each market more than $1 million dollars' worth of product per year.

When people talk about "corporate farming" taking over family farming, this is what they are referring to, but it is not a completely accurate way to understand the situation. Industrial agribusiness does not really want to own any more of the actual production capacity than it absolutely needs, because it is very expensive. Land costs a lot, and the return on investment for the producers of food is for the most part negative. For instance, in the twenty-two-year-span of

1996 to 2017, corn production was only profitable for six of those years.

Appreciation in land value does compensate for the low return in producing crops for sale. This inflation potential can look good as an investment diversification for a billionaire seeking a trophy ranch to feed his passion for hunting. He can play the mighty hunter for a few years, and his heirs can sell the ranch for more than the land originally cost. Increasingly, hedge funds invest in farmland with the expectation that inflation will yield them an eventual profit.

However, for a true family farmer, the point is to pass the land on to future generations. Paying the bank for the purchase of land is, therefore, the largest drain on their finances. Family farmers are in a bind: the financial pressure is to increase the size of the farm in the hope that owning the equipment needed to stay current with the technology can be amortized over more production. More operating costs, more work, more debt.

The problem inevitably comes when the farm passes on to the next generation. If multiple siblings inherit, not all of them can live on the proceeds of the farm. Therefore, one (or more) buys out their brothers and sisters and pays them inflated land prices. The farm now has more debt. In this manner, farmland stays in perpetual debt, and the money that would have circulated in the local community flows instead to the "too big to fail" banks.

What Do Farmers Raise?

If you were to randomly stop people on the streets of any city and ask them what exactly it is that most farmers raise, they would probably think about the food they could buy at the farmers' market: sweet corn, tomatoes, green beans, carrots, kale, apples, and blueberries. Maybe they would also mention eggs from free-range chickens. In reality, less than 1 percent of farmland is devoted to the production of vegetables and a little more than 1 percent to fruits and nuts, for a total of 2.1 percent. Another 13 percent of farmland is used for grains such as wheat, rice, and barley (mostly for beer).

Out of the totality of farmland, some 57 percent is pasture

and hay, devoted to the raising of livestock. As for the remaining 28 percent of total farmland in the United States, it produces corn, soybeans, and a few other field crops primarily used to feed and fatten livestock. Corn and soybeans dominate the Midwest to the extent that corn and soybeans are practically all you can see on a drive through Iowa.

Most, but not all, corn and soybeans go to fattening chickens, hogs, and cows. One-third of the corn crop is used to produce ethanol to be mixed with gasoline. Ten percent of the fuel that you put in your car comes from agriculture. The export of corn, soybean, and wheat accounts for 23 percent of total US exports. The exported wheat, of course, is for human consumption, but the corn and soybeans go to fatten livestock, mostly in Asia. We also directly export beef, pork, and poultry, all of which are fed corn and soybeans. This means that corn, soy, and wheat underpin $50 billion of our annual international trade balance. In 2019, the United States had a negative trade balance of $577 billion. Without agricultural exports, the deficit would be $50 billion worse.[2]

The Economic Reality of Being a Farmer

To understand the situation in agriculture, we need to understand the economic realities faced by farmers. The following example is based on the economic challenges faced by a farm family just starting out.

The USDA tells us that the average farm totals 443 acres. The average value per acre totals $3,100. For this exercise, however, we are going to consider the average-size farm (443 acres) in Iowa, where the average value of cropland suitable for raising corn and soybeans is $7,290 per acre. The purchase cost of this farm would be $3,229,430. To finance this farm at a 5 percent interest rate over 25 years would amount to an annual payment of $226,547.[3] According to the *2019 Indiana Farm Custom Rates*, it costs $441 per acre to plant and harvest a crop of corn.[4] If, however, the farmer is adept at keeping older machinery functioning, these costs can be a little bit less. Therefore, annual operating costs are, at the maximum, $195,363. Add that to the $226,547 loan payment and it comes to a grand total of $421,910, or $952 per acre, to bring in a crop. We can already see from the above example financial numbers, which the average American never sees, that this is a financially precarious proposition. According to a recent article by CNBC, 56 percent of Americans cannot cover a $1,000 emergency with savings.[5]

The USDA tells us that the average yield of a field of corn in Iowa is 176.4 bushels per acre. The average price of corn per bushel as of 2018 was $3.61 per bushel. However, the farmer does not receive the full $3.61, because the cost of transportation to the terminal market is deducted. In the case of Iowa, it can be up to 50 cents per bushel.

You add it all up and you find that the crop is worth $549 per acre for a gross value of $243,207, or $178,703 less than what it has cost to produce. Although a farmer—classified as small by USDA standards—is handling funds that are in the hundreds of thousands of dollars, the farmer's actual income is negative. Beginning farmers can easily be in a worse financial situation than the 56 percent of people who cannot meet a $1,000 financial emergency.

Note that in this thumbnail sketch of the economics of raising corn, this farm had a gross sale under $350,000—the cutoff point, according to the USDA, between small family farms and the medium-size family farms. This hypothetical farm is in today's American agricultural system by no means anything other than modest.

Something else to consider: Every year, the USDA, in order to have a standard baseline, calculates the parity price for each of the major crops. Parity is a ratio that relates the current value of a crop back to what farmers received from 1909 to 1914. The current parity value for a bushel of corn is $13.20. In the past 106 years, the market value of corn has gone down, but costs have increased at the rate of inflation.

A final thing to consider: If our farm family had assets worth $3,229,430 that were invested in stocks and bonds instead of a farm, the annual income at a 5 percent return would be $161,472. The only reason anyone can give for being an active farmer is that the work and cultural lifestyle give great satisfaction. In addition is the realization that if ever the farm is sold, it will be lost to the family forever.

Please note that in the above example, I laid out the economics of raising corn in Iowa. However, all other crops would have similar negative income realities. Farmers are, for the most part, stuck with the limitations of the environment where their farm is located. It is corn in Iowa, wheat in North Dakota, and rice in Louisiana. The high price of the most important input—land—dictates that you must raise the crop most suitable for your environment with the highest potential of coming close to making a profit. The exception would be for irrigated farming in places like the Central Valley of California, where anything can be raised. In that situation, the crop with the highest return per acre would be the logical choice.

It's rational to ask, if a farmer is losing money on every acre of corn harvested, how can farmers possibly stay in business? The short answer is subsidies—personal, federal, and familial. For small family farms, off-farm income is essential. One spouse or the other needs a job, ideally with health benefits. One accident or serious illness would instantly put the whole farm in jeopardy.

Given this untenable situation, farmers like to tell jokes about what it takes to make it in agriculture:

- Have you heard about the agricultural bigamy act for farmers who can't make it with just one wife working in town?
- How do you make a small fortune in farming? You start with a large fortune.
- I lost my ass ranching and now I can't keep my pants up.
- How about the farmer who won the lottery? He said that he would just keep farming until that was gone too.
- The only way to get into farming is to bury your parents or marry a farmer.

Federal subsidies are vital, without which there would be mass bankruptcy. According to the Agriculture Fairness Alliance, farmers received a total of $53 billion—about half of all farm revenues—from

US taxpayers in 2020. Most of this largesse, however, did not flow to the small family farms. Although there are caps on how much any one farm can receive, the largest farms are allowed to structure family corporations so that each family member can qualify separately. For instance, of the $19 billion allocated to agriculture in 2020 through the Coronavirus Aid, Relief, and Economic Security (CARES) Act, the upper limit to any one farmer is $250,000; but the biggest farms usually have multiple partners, and each gets the maximum.

The third, and possibly most beneficial subsidy, is that which a young rancher or farmer gets from their parents. With hard work and some luck, each generation adds a little to the familial equity. The more that can be passed to the younger generation, the better chance they will have to pass on more equity to the generation after them. However, even if you inherit a whole farm or ranch free and clear, it can still be lost through bad luck and bad management. That happened to a neighbor. And as I mentioned earlier, if the farm is to be shared over multiple siblings, the land takes on more debt, not less.

The irony is that because of lower overall debt and off-farm income, many of the 1,820,192 farms that produce less than $350,000 are in better financial shape than the 166,394 large family farms. For larger farms, the off-farm job income is smaller relative to the size of the debt. This makes large farms even more dependent on federal subsidies.

Without government subsidies, food production in America would collapse. This is both an irony and a measure of the duplicity of the philosophy underlying our national farm policy. For most of this past half century the message has been that small farms are inefficient and must be encouraged to go out of business in order for efficient modern farms to thrive. Farmers are fed this message by university economists, lobbyists from the banking industry, global agribusiness, the USDA, and, ultimately, as part of official congressional policy. It is all a big lie.

Get Big or Get Out

Farming in America went through a very rough patch during the Great Depression of the 1930s. In my neck of the woods of eastern Montana (not a whole lot of trees in view), the attrition was severe. People just walked away from farms in which they had invested two or three decades of their lives. The Depression years were compounded by drought. Farmers could raise no crops, and surviving livestock sold for pennies per pound. No one had actual cash. One old-timer told me that he had been able to grow enough potatoes to feed his family, but they had no grease to fry them in. He bought a side of pork from a neighbor and it took him a year to save the dollar to pay that neighbor back. One lesson, as nature reminded us, is that the climate of eastern Montana, along with much of the Great Plains, is simply too severe for the type of agriculture that the homesteaders brought with them from Europe and east of the Mississippi.

My grandparents married and homesteaded in 1913, but my grandfather died in 1920. My grandmother hung on through the 1920s and 1930s, and in 1935, she inherited a small ranch on MacDonald Creek near Grass Range, on the condition that she pay the back taxes. A live stream and good valley soil make the difference between having a viable farm/ranch in eastern Montana or not. This ranch, though small by Montana standards, has good fields and permanent water.

The hills and plains around my ranch are dotted with the remains of homesteads, country schools, and even functioning towns. Lots and lots of dreams dried up in the drought and Depression of the twenties and thirties. Enough time has elapsed that the evidence is buried into the soil. You must know where to look, but there were people trying to scratch out a living everywhere. Following the Great Depression, the more fortunate acquired the better, more productive land that their neighbors sold for next to nothing, and the least desirable land reverted back to the government and is now under the administration of the BLM.

Rural America did not recover from the Depression of the 1930s until the needs of World War II declared agriculture a strategic industry with guaranteed pricing to stimulate production. When the GIs came home, my father among them, they came back to a rural America that was in its best financial shape ever.

In the 1930s, when Steinbeck's Joad family gave up their farm in Oklahoma to find work in California, the United States had 6.8 million farms—the most farms ever in the history of the United States, according to the USDA Economic Research Service. By 1974, we had lost 3.3 million of those family farms. After 1974, the official number decreased by another 1.5 million and has since stayed relatively stable at just over 2 million farms.[6] But as we saw earlier, just over half of the remaining farms own on average 81 acres and produce less than $10,000 worth of food per year. Industrialized agriculture refers to these smallest farms as "hobby farmers." A less condescending way to look at these small farmers would be to note that among them are the conservators of a family farming tradition.

The issue my father, his neighbors, and the US government faced in the 1950s and 1960s was overproduction. The fertility of the farmland in the continental United States simply produced more foodstuffs than the population could consume. The fifties and sixties saw tremendous improvements in yields due to new agricultural technology: fertilizers, pesticides, herbicides, antibiotics, vaccines, and new, more versatile and powerful machinery.

Coming out of the New Deal and World War II, the government had made a commitment to farmers, and to rural America, to ensure basic prosperity. However, overproduction meant that farmers could simply not survive on what "free market" prices offered.

Supply-management schemes were implemented through the national farm bills. In return for fallowing (i.e., not planting) a portion of their fields, farmers received guaranteed prices through a loan program. The government loaned farmers a set amount for each crop so that they would not have to sell until the market price reached that agreed-upon floor price. If the loan price was not exceeded, the government would take possession of the crop and store it. As a result, taxpayers ended up owning mountains of soybeans, corn, and wheat.

In the 1960s, economists and policymakers decided that the problem was not the bountiful farmland but rather the farmers themselves. The Food and Agriculture Act of 1965 made most production controls voluntary and set price supports in relation to world market prices. With this law, Congress essentially abandoned their commitment to keep farm prices at "parity" levels. The orthodox economic doctrine, in essence, became that small farmers were "inefficient," and if government policies fostered attrition in small farms, the resulting larger farms would reach a point of "economy of scale" and these "efficient" large farms would be able to prosper from supply-and-demand market prices.

In other words, agricultural economists measured "efficiency" in farmers per acre—a rather insane metric. As dictated by Earl Butz, US secretary of agriculture under Presidents Richard Nixon and Gerald Ford, the "human resources were removed from agriculture," and by 1974, there were 3.3 million fewer farms in America. Butz's motto was "Get big or get out." Beginning in the late 1960s, successive farm bills sacrificed and emptied rural America of its population. Fewer farms meant fewer people in rural places, resulting in fewer main street businesses, and fewer lower-paying jobs. In essence, rural America was transformed into a very large, sparsely populated, economically depressed zone—a slum of sorts, complete with abandoned farmsteads, decaying trailer homes, and empty towns.

Plant Fencerow to Fencerow

Shortly after I took over the ranch from my parents in 1975, I, along with several local farmers and ranchers, was invited to a dinner and seminar on the future of agriculture. The keynote speaker was the president and CEO of the Chicago Mercantile Exchange, Clayton Yeutter. In 1985, President Ronald Reagan appointed him US trade representative, and in 1989, President George H. W. Bush appointed him US secretary of agriculture. In 1991, Yeutter became chairman of the Republican National Committee.

In the early 1970s, Russia, for the first time, purchased a lot of wheat from the United States. This purchase caught the market off guard, causing prices to spike, opening the idea that the United States could be exporting a lot of the grain that was building up in all the storage bins across the nation.

Yeutter's message was that we would become the world leader in the export of grains—we would feed the world. Farms would be able to grow in size until they were "efficient," and because of export demand, the "market" would take care of us. He encouraged us to buy more land and plant fencerow to fencerow. According to Yeutter, American farmers would dominate the international markets as long as we kept the price of wheat, corn, and soybeans so low that other countries could not compete, forcing the world to buy grain from the United States.

The room exploded with cheering farmers and ranchers. Yeutter was a dynamic speaker, and I learned that day that farmers and ranchers can be a gullible audience. After the speech, I was talking with an older rancher whose opinion I respected and asked him what he thought. He said that Yeutter had just told everyone exactly how he was going to put them out of business, and everyone had just thanked him.

Sure enough, that's what happened. Banks were already pushing easy money, farmers bought land at inflated prices, and by 1980, it all crashed in a cascade of events. Inflation was soaring across the nation, causing the Federal Reserve to increase interest rates. High interest rates had the effect of keeping the value of the dollar high on the world market, just the opposite of what you want if your goal is to export corn, soybeans, and wheat. Farmers who had borrowed heavily found themselves paying 15–18 percent interest rates. Finally, as if inflation was not enough, exports to Russia were banned because the Russians invaded Afghanistan.

The first half of the 1980s were tough, tough times on farmers. Bankers who had been your best buddies turned into vindictive holders of bad debt. Everyone blamed farmers for making bad decisions even though those decisions were based on what the experts and bankers themselves had advised. It was, if you appreciate the irony, the same scenario that this country went through recently with the housing bubble and the resulting Great Recession of 2007–2009. Both economic crises were caused by bad advice from experts and bankers who threw caution to the wind. It was fiduciary malpractice on a massive scale.

The financial crisis of the early 1980s weighed heavily on rural America. Farm foreclosures and suicides were constant. Farmers and ranchers tended to blame themselves as failures; they had not worked hard enough, made bad financial decisions, and let their families down. By the time the farm crisis of the eighties was over, the era of the independent family farm was also over.

But the policy of exporting our way to profitability through marketing cheap grains was not over, and it continues to this day. In the words of sociologist Harwood Schaffer and Daryll Ray, professor emeritus at the University of Tennessee's Institute of Agriculture,

> In ag policy, the zombie idea is that lowering the US price will increase or at least maintain export market share. We saw this with the 1985 Farm Bill where we lowered the loan rate in order to "recapture 'our' export markets." The lower rates were continued in the 1990 Farm Bill with tweaking on providing extra income to farmers.
>
> These changes did not work so we doubled down and adopted the 1996 Farm Bill. . . . Even with these results, many ag economists and politicians continue to repeat the zombie idea that lower crop prices will allow US farmers to increase (or at least maintain) their share of U.S. corn, soybean complex, and wheat markets.[7]

Here we were in 2020, relying on China to buy corn, soybeans, pork, chicken, and beef even though we'd declared a trade war on them. China, however, has other options because the thing that the policymakers and experts back in 1980 failed to consider is that most countries of the world value food sovereignty, because they had all experienced food shortages and famine. China, India, and Southeast Asia used the high-tech agricultural tools pioneered by the United States and Europe to increase the yields of their farm sector. This

Green Revolution was led by agronomist Norman Borlaug, who received the Nobel Prize for his efforts. These countries now regularly export food. Meanwhile, the oligarchs in Brazil partnered with global agribusiness to steal land from Indigenous people and clear the Amazon rain forest to raise corn, soybeans, and cattle—on a massive scale. All for export.

The 1996 farm bill, dubbed the Freedom to Farm Act, (and, by farmers, Freedom to Fail) was lauded as a way to eliminate the need for subsidies. Up until then, subsidies were based on a supply-management system that allocated how many acres of each crop farmers were allowed to plant. The Freedom to Farm Act opted for what they termed flexibility, the assumption being that if farmers were allowed the flexibility to plant the crops they wanted—not just corn, soybeans, or wheat—farm subsidies would no longer be needed.

Instead of receiving checks directly from the government, farmers were required to buy crop insurance to cover losses due to weather. After all, the thinking went, what could be more market efficient than insurance. The premium for the crop insurance is, however, heavily subsidized by the government and the costs for the taxpayers have gone up steadily. One reason for this increase in farm subsidy costs is that private insurance companies are now able to siphon off a stream of taxpayers' money for administering the program, money supposedly meant to support rural America.

The lie in all of this is that the larger farms are not, in fact, more efficient, because the concept of economies of scale is an illusion. Small farmers have yields that match or exceed those of the large. The real problem is the excess production capacity, along with the corporate appropriation of the market infrastructure.

American family farmers have been left holding the bag from the anti-family farm policies of the last sixty years. The American public is also on the hook, because these failed farm policies cost taxpayers more and more. So in 2020, between payments to farmers to compensate for the "trade war" with China and the regular stream of subsidies, including crop insurance, US taxpayers will be out $53 billion.

Is It Neoliberalism or Nouveau Fascism?

As was mentioned earlier, the policies of the 1970s set the stage for the economic conditions for family farms to worsen. The plan to "remove human resources from agriculture," endorsed by university economists and policymakers alike, had nearly met its goals. The policy to dominate world agricultural exports by "planting fencerow to fencerow" was gaining traction. But also hatched was a policy to stop antitrust oversight and regulation of corporate mergers.

This latter policy was not confined to agriculture, making the 1970s the beginning of an assault on democracy itself. As dangerous as Richard Nixon was for America, American economist and statistician Milton Friedman (and former solicitor general of the United States Robert Bork) proved to be far worse. In 1976, Friedman received the Nobel Prize in Economics for his theories on neoliberalism, which "is most commonly associated with laissez-faire economics. In particular, neoliberalism is often characterized in terms of its belief in sustained economic growth as the means to achieve human progress, its confidence in free markets as the most-efficient allocation of resources, its emphasis on minimal state intervention in economic and social affairs, and its commitment to the freedom of trade and capital."[8]

This concept is economic doublespeak, meaning that government should not interfere in the monopolistic tendencies of corporations if it can be argued that consumers were somehow benefiting. Government's role in the economy should be confined to preventing inflation by managing the money supply and preventing wages from increasing. For neoliberals, the "invisible hand of the market" would take care of everything else.

Barry Lynn, researcher, author, and executive director of the Open Markets Institute, points out that as a result of neoliberalism, our government changed from representing us as citizens to considering us to be consumers. He goes on to observe that we "as citizens" also abdicated our responsibilities to actively ensure that government works for our benefit, and accepted instead the passive comforts of being a consumer. The door was open for the corporations to infiltrate the government and appropriate the economy. He likens that process to a coup d'etat.[9]

What Friedman and Bork espoused began to be implemented by the Reagan administration. Paul Volcker was the chairman of the Federal Reserve Board while Clayton Yeutter, whose seminar I had attended, managed trade and agriculture policy. Their time in power was used to free corporations from oversight and regulations. Reagan proclaimed government to be the problem, and many Americans found this inspirational. The goal became to starve government to the point that it could be drowned in a bathtub. Not only would there be no "new" taxes, but there would also be no "old" taxes for the wealthy at least. As for the rest of us, if we wanted roads and schools, we could either pay for them on the local level or do without.

For the wealthiest Americans, taxes were cut again and again as the policies fostering economic equality coming out of World War II were abandoned in a bipartisan assault. In 2010, the US Supreme Court ruled, in the *Citizens United v. Federal Election Commission* case, that there could be no limit on the freedom of speech—in the form of campaign financing—of corporations. The *Citizens United* decision effectively transferred power from American citizens to global corporations. The coup was completed.

If you look in dictionaries, "fascism" has a complex set of definitions; prominent among them is an authoritarian state exploiting extreme nationalism. But embedded within the definitions is the fact that under fascist regimes, there is a very close relationship between the financial elite and the fascist government. Their interests merge. So do you really need an authoritarian head of state mobilizing the forces of the state against a "hated minority" to have a fascist government? Or can you have a "soft" form of fascism—a "nouveau fascism?"

Former president Donald Trump seems to have made a determined effort to be a fascist, authoritarian head of state. He and his partisans proclaimed immigrants to be the "hated minority," and as the 2020 election heated up, socialists—defined as everyone not wearing a MAGA cap—were added to the list. He had already in numerous public rallies declared the press as an "enemy of the people." Perhaps Trump spent too much time playing golf to pull off full-blown fascism, but clearly many of his followers would willingly replace the Constitution with an authoritarian state. However, according to a 2020 CNBC report, Wall Street massively funded the Democratic opposition to Trump.[10] Trump may have caused Wall Street too much turmoil and unpredictability. Perhaps the nouveau fascists understand they do not need an authoritarian fascist state in order to maintain control of the government and the economy.

The original rationale that neoliberal policies were meant to benefit the consumer did not work out very well at all. The Congressional Budget Office reported that, based on 2019 dollars, the average wage for the bottom 90 percent in the nation rose from $30,880 in 1979 to $38,923 in 2019. In contrast, the income of the top 1 percent rose from $291,329 to $758,434 during the same time period. According to the report, the top 1 percent possess 19.5 times more wealth than the bottom 90 percent. The top 0.1 percent, totaling 330,000 individuals, own as much wealth as the bottom 90 percent, which totals 297,000,000 individuals.[11]

Monopolies and the Neoliberal

"Farmers buy retail and sell wholesale" pretty much sums up the economic reality farmers face. Since 1980, when the US Department of Justice stopped enforcing the Sherman Antitrust Act, investigations of collusion between competing agricultural firms have just about stopped. The Clayton Act, which governs the merger of competing firms, also stopped being enforced. To my knowledge, all mergers concerning competing agri-corporate firms have been allowed. The Packers and Stockyards Act, which regulates competition in livestock markets and is overseen by the USDA, has also been ignored.

The result is that, as of 2020, farmers have very limited alternatives for all major purchased inputs and for the marketing of their produce. In the case of the cartel that controls the meat protein market (poultry, hogs, and fat cattle), they have succeeded in almost completely eliminating the transparent public market.

On the input side are the things that farmers must purchase in order to successfully plant and harvest a crop. This ranges from machinery, fertilizer, and chemicals to the technologies vital for the future of agriculture. Farmers are facing oligopolies for all of these essential inputs:

- **Farm equipment:** John Deere, CNH Industrial, and AGCO.
- **Fertilizer:** Nutrien (a merger of Potash Corporation of Saskatchewan and Agrium) and Mosaic (formerly co-owned by Cargill).
- **Seeds:** Corteva, Syngenta (Chinese owned), and Bayer—together they monopolize 60 percent of the US market.
- **Herbicides/pesticides:** Corteva, Syngenta, and Bayer—they also have 60 percent of the US market.
- **Precision agriculture and other emerging technology:** Corteva, Syngenta, and Bayer.[12]

As we see above, the market for seeds and chemicals is dominated by the same three companies. Corteva is the result of a 2017 merger of the chemical giants Dow Chemical and DuPont. Bayer and Monsanto merged in 2018 and kept the name of the German chemical giant Bayer. Syngenta was a Swiss company bought in 2016 by the Chinese government through the China National Chemical Corporation. Between them, these three global giants control 60 percent of the US market, including all of what is termed the genetically modified organism (GMO) seed technology.

These three corporations are also poised to control the future of industrial agricultural production through domination of "precision agriculture," or "precision ag." This concept includes a grouping of high-tech innovations using satellite and drone surveillance to accurately map soils and monitor plant growth across fields. Instead of treating a field as a single unit, seed, fertilizer, herbicide, and pesticide placement is calibrated to the needs of different areas of the field, such as variations in soil types. The promise is to target seed, fertilizer, herbicide, and pesticide requirements just to where they are most needed, reducing the overall amounts required.

Added to this concept is the increased utilization of robotized machinery. Self-driving tractors, seeders, and sprayers are increasingly controlled by the surveillance data. In addition, harvesters automatically monitor the yields in real time to verify the results of the precision ag. It seems a bit dubious that companies that are in the business of selling seeds, herbicides, and pesticides will be advising farmers on how little of each to use.

Presumably, precision ag technology and services will be proprietary systems, so that farmers will have to choose which company to align themselves with. This will result in even less independence and will put farmers further down the path to complete vertical integration, where they are increasingly reliant on a single corporation for inputs, technology, and marketing of production—in which case there will be a complete loss of market independence.

On the commodity selling side of things, farmers must sell to the following cartels:

- **Corn**: Archer Daniels Midland (ADM), Bunge, Cargill, Ingredion, and the Louis Dreyfus Company (Dreyfus) together purchase 87 percent of the US crop.
- **Soybean**: ADM, Bunge, Cargill, and Ag Processing together purchase 85 percent of US crop.
- **Cattle**: Cargill, JBS Foods (Brazilian owned), Tyson Fresh Meats, and National Beef (co-owned by Marfig Global Foods—also Brazilian) together slaughter 85 percent of the US fat cattle.
- **Pork**: Tyson, JBS, and Smithfield (Chinese owned) together control 70 percent of US hogs.
- **Chicken**: Tyson, JBS, Sanderson Farms, Perdue—control 50 percent of US chickens.[13]

An oligopoly is a cartel of firms that controls the sale of things, while an oligopsony is a cartel of firms that controls the purchase of things. In both cases, the competitiveness of the market is compromised and

America's farmers are hemmed in from both sides. In some instances, farmers are subject to both phenomena by the same corporation. This is the case with Cargill, which is dominant in both the sale of fertilizers and the purchase of corn and soybeans. Cargill goes one step further and is one of the four firms that controls beef-packing.

Cargill, Bunge, and Dreyfus are unique in that they are very old family-owned firms that, between them, control much of the international trade in grains. Cargill was founded in 1865 and is the largest privately held corporation in America. The Louis Dreyfus Company was founded in 1851 in France and accounts for about 10 percent of the global trade in agricultural products. Bunge Corporation started as Bunge and Born in 1818 in the Netherlands. This company is especially dominant in South America in the international soybean trade.

These firms control the market by controlling access to the transportation of the commodities. Corn, soybeans, wheat, and rice move in massive quantities by barge on the Mississippi River or by rail to ports on the Gulf, East, and West Coasts. By owning the facilities that load the barges and railcars, along with the facilities that transfer the cargo to ships, Cargill, Bunge, and Dreyfus effectively control the international market for these commodities.

The news often reports that American farmers have made a major export sale, which is not true at all, because farmers do not sell anything to any foreign buyer. Cargill et al. makes the sale and, more often than not, presells the crop, because their global information network allows them to understand both the supply and the demand better than any farmer or government could ever hope to.

Earlier in this essay, I made the observation that only 209,007 farms produce 78.7 percent of sales. One reason for this fact is that the agri-cartels find it more convenient to deal in large quantities of production. For instance, procuring chickens a few dozen at a time from hundreds of chicken farmers is, for them, more inconvenient than sending a semitrailer to pick up thousands of chickens from a factory farm. Ultimately, what we as citizens and consumers need to consider is whether this efficiency in scale warrants the environmental risks, the social dislocations, and the vulnerabilities to the supply chain.

Chickens

In my grandmother's day, the market for chickens, eggs, milk, cream, and butter was all local. There were small businesses in each community that slaughtered chickens, bottled milk, and made butter. These commodities, in turn, were distributed through local grocery stores. Every family farm in America did a side business in eggs, chickens, milk, and/or cream. This was the cash income that housed, clothed, and fed the family.

Today, however, just a handful of firms control the slaughter and wholesaling of chicken, pork, and beef. These same firms have major stakes in two or all three of these production chains. Tyson and JBS are dominant in all three meat protein sources. Note Cargill again in beef. This brings us to a discussion of the role of Concentrated Animal Feeding Operations (CAFOs; i.e., factory farms) and contract farming.

The Tyson family pioneered the CAFO system in chicken. Adverse weather is the major risk in growing and fattening livestock. The more the environment can be controlled, the better the potential for fast, efficient growth of the animal in question. The Tyson solution was to move the entire egg-to-fryer cycle indoors. Tyson went one step further and contracted with farmers to raise the chickens while Tyson retains ownership and provides the feed. The contract farmer is paid based on the number and weight of chickens delivered back to Tyson.

Tyson and the other chicken integrators promise an attractive yearly income on the condition that the contract grower invests in a state-of-the-art chicken house and meticulously follows the company's expert advice. The banks and the chicken company work in concert. The company offers a contract as a precondition for the bank to approve the loan to build the chicken house.

The problem for the farmer comes when something happens to the chickens under their care. Tyson not only outsources the labor necessary to raise chickens but also outsources the risk. If a disease should wipe out an entire chicken house, Tyson is out the minimal cost of the original chicks and whatever feed had gone into them.

The contract growers are out all of their labor and the cost of heating and cooling the chicken house, disposal of the manure, and, in the case of a disaster, disposal of the dead birds. With no income for that cycle, farmers cannot pay the bank. Contract growers are locked into a system that is essentially the sharecropping of chickens, in which they have no control over the marketing side of things. The contracts are written so that Tyson and the other poultry firms have no obligations to their captive growers.

Contract chicken farmers who have been burned by the poultry industry, such as Benny Bunting from North Carolina, liken Tyson's innovation as being a "serf on our own land."[14] The problem for the contract grower is compounded because each company that offers contracts is strategically located. If a grower initially signs up to raise chickens for Tyson, they cannot switch to Perdue because Perdue will not have facilities in your area.

From the perspective of the chicken company, the system is brilliant. Each slaughter plant has a cadre of captive growers. These captive growers have made the major financial investments needed to raise chickens, so the company is not burdened by having to pay interest on a low-return aspect of the chicken-raising business. If something happens to the chickens, the company is not out much. If the market for finished chickens is soft, the company is not contractually obligated to supply the grower with chicks or feed. The major portion of all the financial risks has, therefore, been transferred to the party who has the least ability to object.

In the system that Tyson pioneered, the overall public market for chickens disappeared because the infrastructure for processing chickens on a local level also disappeared. The local foods movement is trying to reconnect the farmer directly with the consumer, but the problem they face is that the market infrastructure that made that process efficient must also be re-created. This is the reason that food at the farmers' market is relatively expensive. The work of aggregating, processing, transporting, and marketing the food is not economically efficient because of this lack of appropriately scaled processing and marketing infrastructure.

In an economic sense, what Tyson pioneered is highly efficient.

Chickens are raised in an environmentally controlled setting. They have been genetically selected to grow as fast as possible. The feed is calibrated to optimize growth. Disease is a risk, but, when necessary, chicken barns are isolated from outside contaminants and workers' access is tightly controlled. The chickens are whisked from the barns to the slaughter plants, where they fly through killing and disassembly by a workforce of largely underpaid immigrants with no ability to advocate for their own interests. From there, the chickens end up on the supermarket shelves in packages designed for the convenience of every possible consumer. If you don't like eating all the parts of a chicken, you can purchase just the pieces that you prefer. If you don't like cooking chicken at all, you can buy roasted or fried chicken. And this is all done for a relatively cheap price.

What the consumer does not have to pay for are the externalities. Each chicken barn produces a mountain of chicken manure. Since the barns are geographically concentrated, they collectively produce more chicken manure than the surrounding fields can absorb. Overapplication of chicken manure risks having a rainstorm wash it into the rivers, contaminating the downstream water supply and, in the case of the mouth of the Mississippi, killing the fish and shrimp in a gigantic floating dead zone.

The work in a chicken disassembly plant is demanding and brutal. Communities that welcomed the plants as a source of economic development are paying the price. The local people who were initially hired but had alternative employment opportunities soon quit. Tyson and the other chicken companies then recruited the aforementioned immigrant workers.

Often the chicken company hires these workers through a contractor who conveniently does not always carefully check the workers' immigration papers. Again the risk, in this case fines for employing undocumented workers, is outsourced, because the labor contractor is liable, not the company. The work is harsh and injuries numerous, especially disabilities due to repetitive injuries, such as carpal tunnel syndrome. When people can no longer work, they are put out on the streets to live from what the public assistance system may or may not provide. For the communities that were counting on economic development, the costs of a chicken plant have often proven to be expensive.

As for the consumers, they are getting inexpensive chicken. But there are also some externalities at their level too. We are warned by government food experts to treat each chicken as a toxic source of contamination. They tell us to wash our hands and sterilize the countertop after handling raw chicken. Then there is a matter of the flavor of factory farm chicken. If you have never eaten a farm-raised, free-range chicken, you have no idea what a chicken is supposed to taste like.

What we haven't talked about are the chickens themselves. Are they being humanely housed, raised, handled, and slaughtered? There are reasons to doubt all four of those points. The bottom line is that what Tyson created is a system based on exploitation of every aspect of the chicken business. The chickens, the environment, the growers, the workers, and the consumers are all sacrifice points. Then to bring the conversation around to the corn and soybeans that make up the ration for the chickens, none of this system designed to supply cheap food is possible without corn and soybeans being sold for less than the cost of producing it.

Some statistics as of 2019, courtesy of the National Chicken Council, offer further context: There are approximately 30 firms in the chicken business, 4 of whom control 50 percent of the business. But there are now only 25,500 contract growers. In 2019, there were 9.2 billion broiler chickens raised and marketed, which means that, on average, each contract grower raised 360,000 chickens. The chicken companies employ 350,000 workers directly and another 1.2 million indirectly. The wholesale value of the chickens is $65 billion, while the retail value is $95 billion. Sixteen percent of the broilers raised in the United States are exported.[15]

What is not mentioned by the National Chicken Council is that the contract grower receives about 5 cents per pound, which is 30 cents for a 6-pound chicken. For that wage, the grower must house, feed, and clean up behind the chickens. But assuming the financial risk is also a significant liability and potentially costly. According to the *WATT PoultryUSA* magazine, in 2015, US poultry producers lost 50 million chickens to highly pathogenic avian influenza.

Avian influenza, which originated in Asia, keeps circulating and mutating among the Asian continent's chicken industry. Some strains can even infect humans, which is a major worry for epidemiologists. But chickens are not the only animals at risk. China has not recovered from an African swine fever (ASF) epidemic and is currently suffering a resurgence of that disease.[16] ASF is 100 percent fatal to swine and is believed to have killed 40 percent of all of the pigs in China. Reports from the USDA Foreign Agricultural Service show that in 2018 there were 441 million head of swine in China, meaning that by 2020 China had lost 176 million pigs to this epidemic, which, incidentally, is twice as many pigs as are raised in the United States.[17]

In 2013, the US pork industry was hit by porcine epidemic diarrhea virus, which is a type of coronavirus, like COVID-19. In that epidemic, 8 million (10 percent of all pigs in the United States) died. The global nature of the industrial factory farm system of raising poultry and hogs puts the entire world at risk of devastating epidemics, some of which can jump from animals to humans.

The cattle industry is not immune to these issues either. Following the ratification of the North American Free Trade Agreement (NAFTA) in 1994, we began to import live cattle from Canada and with them came bovine spongiform encephalopathy (BSE), more commonly known as mad cow disease. Cows in the United States never actually had BSE, but since all cows exhibiting the disease originated in Canada, due to the NAFTA treaty, the United States shared Canada's disease status, which affected US beef exports and, therefore, prices received by ranchers. Although US cattle ranchers did not share in any of the profits from the import of Canadian cattle, we shared their disease and financial risks. BSE was not the only gift from NAFTA; Mexican cattle with bovine tuberculosis are being imported, causing incidents of this disease in the United States. Prior to NAFTA, bovine TB had been nearly eradicated.[18]

The global meat cartel's priorities continually override the well-being of US producers and citizens alike. For instance, we now import fresh beef from Brazil and Namibia, both of which have ongoing foot-and-mouth disease (FMD) epidemics. Should FMD be introduced in the United States through contaminated meat, the results would be economically devastating.

Even the fact that beef is being imported and sold at retail is being hidden from consumers. In 2015, at the urging of the meat cartel, Congress eliminated the requirement for Country of Origin Labeling for beef and pork. Everything else that is imported, from underwear to lamb and seafood, must be labeled. Only beef and pork are exempt, and to compound the deception, if the imported meat is repackaged for retail, it qualifies for a "Product of USA" designation.

Pigs

Unlike chickens, which began to be monopolized and vertically integrated as early as the 1960s, the public competitive market for hogs was not compromised until the 1990s. According to the USDA, 1,057,570 farms raised hogs in 1965. By 1985, that number had dropped by two-thirds. In 2017, the total number of hog producers totaled 66,439. Forty firms own two-thirds of the breeding herd and contract with feeders to fatten the little pigs. In turn, these 40 firms sell the fat hogs to Tyson, JBS, and Smithfield, who kill and market 70 percent of all hogs.[19]

The raising of hogs is a two-stage process. Not until baby pigs are weaned do they go into the growing/fattening stage. This is, of course, also true for chickens. However, hens lay eggs every day, the eggs go into incubators, and twenty-one days later a chick is hatched. Raising baby pigs is a longer, more expensive process. Each sow can farrow two times a year, giving birth, on average, to eight or nine little piglets.

Baby pigs are small (3–4 pounds) and sows huge (300–500 pounds). Sows can very easily lay on and smother the babies. For this reason, under the factory farm system, a sow is kept in a small pen during the time when she has piglets, where she can only stand or lie down but not turn around. The little pigs have shelters to the sides, where they can avoid being smothered by their mother's bulk.

Little pigs are weaned after only 21 days and are then moved to the growing/fattening barn.

The factory farm system of growing/fattening pigs has settled on a barn large enough to hold 2,480 hogs in a building 101 by 93 feet, giving each pig 3.8 square feet. A state-of-the-art confinement hog barn currently costs $800,000.[20] As in the case of the chicken contract growers, the banks require that a prospective hog grower have a contract with a hog integrator. As part of the deal, the prospective contract grower must show that they have sufficient land on which to spread the manure. As with the chicken system, the farmer assumes the risk for losses during the growing phase and for any effluent that may end up in the rivers. Also, as with the chicken system, if the market for pigs goes down, the firms that control the slaughter and retail can cut back on the number of pigs allocated to the contract growers, reducing the growers' overall annual income. The banks, however, still get paid.

Prior to the 1990s, raising and fattening pigs was an independent business in which hog farmers sold their animals in a competitive market to local slaughter plants. Raising hogs was a choice for farmers based on the market price for corn versus the presumed profit for feeding pigs. That age-old system collapsed in just a decade's time. In 1992, only 5 percent of hogs were raised on contract. By 2004, 61 percent were raised on contract. In 1999, 35.8 percent of slaughter hogs were still sold in a spot market. By 2006, only 10.2 percent were publicly priced.[21]

How markets function is critical to how an industry and, ultimately, society is structured. Auction markets in which there are a number of sellers and a number of bidders is the most equitable method to determine the actual value of what is being sold and bought. Other forms of price discovery, such as a negotiated price between the seller of an agricultural commodity and the prospective buyer, favor the buyer over the seller. A negotiated spot market that covers only 10.2 percent of the actual production, but from which the other 89.8 percent of the production is priced, does not meet the standards of a free and fair market in anyone's imagination. It is a market system designed by and for the benefit of the cartel controlling the slaughter and wholesale of pork.

As with chickens, the independent public market for hogs has been made to disappear. You can raise as many chickens and hogs as you might like, but you cannot sell them commercially unless you are aligned with one of the cartel firms that controls the slaughter and wholesale. The "buy local" / farmers' market movement is an attempt to circumvent the cartel and sell to the consumer directly. In so doing, however, participants must re-create a market infrastructure that has disappeared.

In essence, each "free range" chicken and "pasture" hog producer who is selling to a local market becomes a vertically integrated farm-to-retail enterprise. The problem is that this is a costly and time-consuming way to market. The chicken and hog cartels set a very low floor price for what consumers are accustomed to paying in a supermarket. Producers at a farmers' market must sell at a premium in order to compensate for the extra work and expense that went into not only raising but slaughtering, processing, and marketing broiler chickens or hams.

Because the market structures that historically connected producers and consumers no longer exist, the buy-local system is inefficient and expensive, hindering the growth of these alternative markets. The problem is that once an alternative market becomes large enough to attract the attention of the cartel, it is easy for the cartel to undercut and take over. If one questions whether the cartels are interested in preventing the growth of alternative markets, one only needs to look at the efforts to which they go to control the definition of marketing terms such as "natural," "organic," or "free range." What the consumer imagines is a free-range chicken is not necessarily what the corporations have lobbied the government to define as "free range." According to retired extension poultry specialist at Oregon State University Jim Hermes, USDA guidelines require that free-range chickens "have access to the outside. It doesn't mean they go outside, it means they have access. So, in essence, if you have a chicken house with a door where the birds could go outside if they so choose, then by definition they are free range."[22]

Cattle

Just as we have seen in the hog industry, the cattle business is also conducted in two stages. However, for cattle, the two stages are much more separated. A cow has only one calf a year. It takes six to seven months to raise a calf to weaning (550–650 pounds). Then there is another eight or nine months to feed the calf to slaughter weight (1,250–1,400 pounds).

Unlike chickens and pigs, cows are herbivores. This means that for much of their lives, they graze grass, a food source that humans cannot consume. It is in the finishing phase that they are fed high-energy rations of corn and soybeans to accelerate their growth and fat deposition. The mother cows, in the meantime, spend their lifespan of ten to twelve years grazing in the plains, hills, and mountains where other forms of agriculture are not possible.

This long interval between calf crops results in an industry effectively split into two separate systems with separate markets. The packing cartel does not really want to directly control the cow/calf part of the cattle business, because the infrastructure (i.e., land) and labor requirements are just too expensive. However, the feedlot half of the cattle business is conducive to vertical integration; over the past three decades, cattle feeders have been effectively brought under full vertically integrated control beholden to just one packer. The few farmer/feeders left who attempt to feed cattle on an independent basis are finding it increasingly difficult to market their fat cattle at a price that results in a net profit.

Chief executive officer of the Ranchers-Cattlemen Action Legal Fund United Stockgrowers of America Bill Bullard explains the issues facing the cattle industry:

> As meatpackers continually coax feedlots to opt into captive supply arrangements, particularly formula-priced contracts, to avoid market access risk, the cattle industry's price discovery market (i.e., the cash or spot market) grows dangerously thin. So thin, in fact, that its shrinking volume is increasingly insufficient to discover a competitive price

for fed cattle, even though it continues to serve as the determinant of the base price for the growing volume of cattle procured through formula contracts. And, worse, the ultra-thin price discovery market is highly susceptible to meatpacker manipulation.[23]

The statistics on cattle raisers follow the same pattern as they did for chicken and pork producers, except in the case of the cow/calf producers, who have had less severe attrition. There are currently some 729,000 cow/calf producers, down from 1,272,950 in 1980. However, 69,000 of these raise more than 100 cows, while the majority, 660,000 farms, have just a few head. The labor involved in the cow/calf sector makes it difficult for one family to manage more than a few hundred head. Granted there are huge ranches that run herds with thousands of cows, but they need significant numbers of hired hands. The labor requirement is somewhere between 100 to 400 head of mother cows per full-time worker.

In the feedlot sector, the attrition from 1996 to 2012 showed a regular drop from just over 110,000 feedlots to 75,000. However, in 2013 there was a precipitous exit of 45,000 independent feedlot operations to just under 30,000 operations still feeding cattle. The seven largest feedlot concerns together feed 35 percent of the total.[24] These dominant feedlots are only independent from the packers in a technical sense, as they are aligned with one of the dominant packers through the "formula-priced contract" system described above. The hold that packers have over feeders is in scheduling the kill. Every day that a pen of fat cattle is delayed is a day that eats into the very thin margins made by feeding cattle. It is estimated that, given current trends, only 60 vertically integrated mega-feedlots will survive.

Although the cow/calf sector is nominally independent—the last independent sector of mainstream agriculture—the prices bid are more and more dictated by the packing cartel. The big feedlots know their costs of feeding, and they have a pretty good idea of what they will be offered for their fat cattle. They dare not bid too much for the feeder calves needed for their feedlots.

Dairy

There was a time when the policy in the United States was to have dairies surrounding each urban center, supplying consumers with fresh milk, cream, and butter. There were production controls put on dairy farmers regarding how much milk they could sell, and they were guaranteed a base price in return. The goal was to match production with the demand. This arrangement was anathema to the neoliberals, who preached that the market should dictate the price of dairy products, not the government. Apparently, only defense contractors and "too big to fail" banks are exempt from this rule.

As with the other crops and commodities, once the neoliberals got hold of farm policy, the family-size dairy farms very rapidly disappeared. According to the USDA, in 1987 there were 200,000 dairy farms scattered across America. Half of those farms had less than 100 head of cows. As of 2019, we have 34,183 dairies with half of those milking more than 1,300 head. The trend to increased dairy size is not over. The largest dairy in America is in Illinois and milks 30,000 cows. However, the largest dairies in the world are in China, with at least two that milk 40,000 head. Dairy production has centralized, with California milking one-fifth of all cows. Wisconsin is number two but declining, and Idaho is now number three. California and Idaho specialize in large dairies that milk up to 5,000 head of cows each.[25] These are located on irrigation projects where alfalfa is raised for the cows. In the case of California, irrigation relies on a massive canal infrastructure that funnels nearly all of the water out of the Sierra Nevada mountains to water the Central Valley. When runoff water is in short supply, as it has been in recent years, farmers pump from the aquifer below the valley. This has resulted in the subsidence of the entire valley by as much as twenty feet.

I bring this up because what we have done in this nation is convert a dispersed form of agricultural production to one that is concentrated and dependent on water resources that are under threat and much more suited to raising vegetables and fruit. While the water resources of California are being used on crops to feed cows, the hills and valleys of Wisconsin, other midwestern states, and New England are growing back into brush and trees. The manure from these animals, rather than being a resource valuable to farming, becomes a public hazard that has contaminated lettuce grown downstream in the irrigation system, sickening thousands of consumers.

There is another issue to consider. For instance, should there be an earthquake in California damaging the irrigation canal systems, 20 percent of the milk production of the United States would be jeopardized instantly. In the name of neoliberal free-market dogma, we have put many of our milk bottles in one basket. Prudence would say that with an industry as important as our food supply, we should not be dependent on just a handful of sources. But prudence and economic dogma are not necessarily compatible.

But there is more wrong in the dairy industry than just oversize dairies. Family-size dairy farmers tried to protect their market access by forming co-ops. However, these co-ops were taken over by the hired management, who merged the co-ops into bigger and bigger conglomerates. The four largest of these co-ops control 50 percent of the milk. Only about a quarter of the co-op's profits are paid back to the farmer-members. The rest is siphoned off by the executives.

The reality in today's dairy industry is that even though the individual dairies are very large, they are not independent in how they market the milk. Just as in other aspects of agriculture, the market is controlled by a cartel.

Retail

Lest you mistakenly believe that on the retail grocery level you buy in an open competitive market, think again! Walmart, Kroger, Albertsons, and Costco control 45 percent of the retail market. If you say you don't shop at any of those stores, you should check on the internet. City Market, Food 4 Less, Fred Meyer, Smith's Food and Drug, and twelve other brand-name stores are owned by Kroger. As for Albertsons, it owns about twenty store brands, including Safeway and Vons.

In addition, the food choices offered in the stores are not as numerous as you might think. Kellogg, General Mills, and Post market 83 percent of the cold cereals. Four firms led by Coca-Cola market 82 percent of what is offered for soft drinks. Four firms market 77 percent of the beer. Another four firms produce 58 percent of the bread. Cartels surround us in every aspect of the food industry. A start-up competing firm has difficulty acquiring retail shelf space in this system controlled by the supermarket cartel and the monopoly food suppliers.[26]

Market Competition

The reason that we have antitrust laws is not to punish anyone for being successful but to protect competition. When a firm becomes too dominant, it is easier for it to profit by exploiting suppliers, workers, consumers, and the environment rather than providing a superior product.

In the context of agriculture, individual farmers are in competition against each other, not in the sense that two tennis players compete—"I win, you lose"—but in the sense of being innovative to do the job of producing food better. And that spirit of competition extends to all those who are involved in the production of food, from the university agronomist to the people who make and sell machinery and parts, the people who supply services, the people who buy the produce and prepare it for retail, and the retailers themselves.

It is through market competition that a society and its economy grows in a healthy, dynamic fashion. However, when an industry becomes monopolized and vertically integrated, all innovation is filtered through a single board of directors. The first question becomes "How can we profit?" If the innovation does not profit the investors, it does not happen. Incentive and dynamism slows and eventually stops all together.

Within this dissuasion, we should consider the term *price discovery*, which is the process of determining the price of a product through the interactions of buyers and sellers. We Americans take pride in calling ourselves a capitalist country and in the idea that the "free market" drives our economy, without ever really looking at the reality. And that reality is less and less than what one would characterize as an economy driven by free and fair competition.

In agriculture, the power dynamic is skewed against farmers. One must understand that the structure of modern American agriculture is not an accident of natural evolution imposed by the laws of economics. It is no accident that 209,007 farms produce 78.7 percent of the food. Rather, it is the result of policy that allows a handful of corporations to dominate the sale of agricultural inputs and another handful to control the market for what is produced.

Economists in the major universities sanctified the destruction of family farms. The agribusiness corporations fill the halls of Congress with armies of lobbyists advocating for policies that favor their domination of markets. These same corporations cultivate the upper echelons of USDA and promise to reward civil servants with attractive positions once their period of public service comes to an end. Policymakers receive generous campaign contributions in order to pass laws beneficial to the industrialized, corporate model of agriculture.

What to Do About It All

The good news is that the United States has the land base to produce more food than is needed. The bad news is: the climate is getting increasingly unpredictable, with more violent extremes. Disruptions to farming are becoming more and more serious. In 2019, floods along the Mississippi and Ohio River complex drowned millions of acres. In 2020, a freak wind flattened 38 million acres of corn and soybeans in Iowa and adjoining states; meanwhile, five hurricanes in a row slammed into the Gulf Coast, drowning crops. California continues to grapple with drought and fire.

Unpredictability in weather is disastrous to the timing of planting and harvesting crops. In agriculture, you do not have the luxury of waiting until tomorrow. The seeds must be in the ground when they must be, and if the weather keeps you out of the fields, then you have a problem. As the old saying goes, "You make hay when the sun shines."

As we have demonstrated, American agriculture is now securely dominated by globally interconnected agro-industry. Decision-making is centralized into the hands of a relatively small number of global investors whose priorities are to further their own interests, not the interests of the nation or the world's inhabitants.

There is a third area of bad news. The different constituencies, all of whom are people who eat food, have very different opinions about what to do or *not do* about any of it. Consumers are generally not well informed or organized. Propaganda, otherwise known as advertising, confuse the issues in favor of influencing the purchase of certain foods over others. Decision-makers are subject to conflicting demands, often financial. University experts cannot be trusted to be impartial and unbiased. Farmers are also not particularly helpful sources of reliable information, as they tend to look at only their particular situation, not the bigger picture. It is not easy to separate the facts from deliberate falsehoods or from faddish belief systems. Food is a subject on which everyone has an opinion that is often not reliable.

What to Do

The problem, in a nutshell, stems from the fact that the United States has historically had the capability to raise too much corn and soybeans, and still does. This contributes to much of the negative issues that one can identify in the structure of agriculture. The question that needs to be considered is if the current structure of agriculture is sufficiently resilient to adapt to increasing climatic instability and the resulting political and economic dysfunction.

There are many who will argue that modern agriculture is the most productive and efficient as it could possibly be, the most bountiful in all of history. On their side of the argument are tons of economic research papers based on mountains of statistics. But these do not answer the question of whether this system of global-industrial vertical and horizontal integration of agriculture has the ability to adapt to serious market shocks, which will inevitably occur as we increasingly experience dramatic climatic swings. Disruptions and scarcity of food will, in turn, trigger global insurrection and increased movement of economic refugees. This is already happening and can only get worse.

Let me get back to this central question in a meandering way. I have had the privilege to attend a number of the Farm Aid concerts. They are wonderful shows and I encourage everyone to attend. You will not be disappointed by the generous genius of the artists, and the funds raised by Farm Aid go to support family-based agriculture. However, one aspect has always bugged me: the characterization of farmers as a downtrodden class deserving of pity and economic charity. How can people who have sizable investments in land, machinery, and livestock be considered needy? I am not being deliberately unsympathetic—after all, my ranch fits within the midrange of the smaller cohort of family farms. It is most certainly a personal and family tragedy to lose a farm that has been in the family for generations.

Farmers, however, are only underprivileged in the sense that they are being exploited for doing a vital job, and that exploitation results in outcomes that are arguably detrimental to the interests of the nation as a whole. It is, in a sense, less about the individual farmers than it is about the structure of the system. To be sure, other businesses have been disadvantaged by changes in the structure of our economy. For instance, the mom-and-pop grocers disappeared when supermarkets moved into the town. They worked just as hard as farmers and preformed a service just as important.

What I have on trial here is the current structure of agriculture versus the structure as it was in the 1950s. I am not advocating for the same level of technology that existed in the fifties. Modern agrotechnology is not size dependent. However, farms in the fifties bought inputs from and sold production into a local/regional market system. There were many thousands of markets, not just a handful controlled by the agri-cartels that now operate on a global level. The result was that money stayed and circulated within the community instead of being sucked up by the global financial system.

Farms in the fifties were also more diversified and thereby more flexible in their cropping decisions. Flexibility is a key issue. There is an old adage in farming that the "best fertilizer is the farmer's footprints." How can a corporate executive, reading reports from field agents, make appropriate decisions in the time frame necessary to get a crop into the ground during adverse weather conditions? In a sense, this is what the Soviet Union attempted in its centrally planned and controlled collective farm system. The result was disastrous.

There are different movements in this country that are advocating for changes in agricultural production, but they tend to get fixated on a particular pet peeve. I am sure many of you have heard the argument that we should not be raising corn to feed to livestock when that corn could more efficiently be feeding people directly. There are variations on this notion, such that we should not be raising animals in confinement and that if we really need to eat hamburgers, there are vegetarian or cell-cultured alternatives. This argument, in turn, gets tied up with the belief that cows are uniquely guilty of emitting greenhouse gases and are, therefore, a major contributor to global warming.

I'll go at these arguments in reverse order:

Four: Cows emit no more CO_2 or methane than other ruminants—domestic or wild. All other animals and insects that consume cellulose emit these gases because they are the by-product of the digestion of cellulose by microorganisms that reside in their guts. It is an underpinning concept of the science of biology that if grasslands exist, some kind of life-form will expand its population to consume that food source. Suppressing cattle will do nothing to reduce greenhouse gases.

Three: If you feel that a product processed in a factory by subjecting beans and corn to various chemical transformations, so that it looks and tastes like meat, is a more healthful alternative to real beef, then be my guest. The same can be said for the cell-cultured variety of fake meat. The meat protein cells in question are grown in vats of growth hormones and antibiotics. Whatever might be one's prejudice against beef, at least the only ingredient listed on the label is beef.

Two: There are most assuredly ethical issues surrounding the factory farm system of raising animals. But determining the humaneness of the factory farm production is a complicated matter. Chickens, hogs, and cattle have different emotional needs than humans. Anthropomorphizing those needs is not useful.

The one need these animals have in common is food. They are happy when there is abundant food right there in front of their snouts. Also, for the most part, they are not necessarily uncomfortable living in their own wastes. They don't like to be belly deep in wet and cold manure, but as long as it is dry, most animals are content. In pasture conditions, both cattle and sheep seek out and bed in the places that they had previously used as a bed-ground. The manure builds up and provides a kind of fluffy mattress.

These animals all feel more comfortable in a crowd. The ethical questions are "What is too much of a crowd? At what point does crowding become emotionally stressful?" In recent years, there have been regulations requiring that chickens be allowed more space, particularly laying hens. Is this a good thing? Probably. Finally, all these animals do not like to be frightened. The less you do that frightens them, the better. Based on videos I have seen on how chickens are rounded up for their last ride, some of the current practices seem to be problematic, and possibly unethical, and inhumane.

We should also consider the ethical question of providing people with inexpensive food. Whatever one thinks about the ethics of factory farming, the economics speak in the factory farm's favor. Cheap feed grains coupled with an exploitative production and market system result in inexpensive hamburgers, hotdogs, and fried chicken. And this is not just a phenomenon happening in America. China raises four times more pigs than we do, and the Chinese feed them with grains from Brazil and the United States. Factory farm–raised chickens are available in every country, resulting in inexpensive roast chicken available from street vendors in almost all the poorer places of the world.

How then does one balance the ethics? Certainly, a food production system whose efficiency stems from the exploitation of everyone who works in that system, and of the land and animals from which that food is derived, should not be considered ethical. Most probably, the confined raising of livestock will not go away, but it can be done within smaller units, more dispersed on the landscape, with each animal allocated more space. For all of this to happen, it would require the reinstitution of local markets and processing capabilities. What would be lost in exploitive economic efficiencies would be gained in more dynamic local economies.

One: As for feeding less corn to animals and more directly to people, it is not clear that people want to eat that much corn. We are talking about a lot of corn. According to the USDA, in 2018, the national corn crop amounted to 14,420,101,000 bushels (a bushel of corn weighs 56 pounds). This was produced from 81,740,000 acres—primarily from Iowa and the states in the Midwest. To really understand the magnitude, however, you need to factor in soybeans, because corn and soybeans are commonly raised on alternative years and together make up the rations for livestock. Again, in 2018, there were 4,428,150,000 bushels of soybeans harvested from 87,594,000 acres.[27]

I only bring this up because if we are not feeding corn and soybeans to livestock, using a third of the corn crop to produce ethanol, and exporting the rest, what would we be doing with it? Alternatively, what else would we raise on 169,334,000 acres of the most fertile land in the world?

Markets

Given that the United States has excess agricultural capacity, why should there be a concern or even a need for any change? The problem is that each crop has very specific technical requirements: different inputs, different machinery, different market chains. Because agriculture operates on yearly cycles, it is not easy to switch from one crop to another in response to adverse weather conditions. Farmers have, in essence, been forced to put all their eggs in one basket when in reality they need to be able to diversify their cropping strategy. What industrial monoculture agriculture has done is eliminate alternative production and market chains. If you are in Iowa and the crop is not corn or soybeans, where are you going to sell it? For that matter, where are you going to get the seed? Where are you going to get the machinery to plant and harvest the crop?

Then, too, we must not forget that markets for the major commodities are global. What happens in Europe, South America, or Asia has repercussions in North America and vice versa. Climate change is happening everywhere and in ways that are unpredictable. Maybe in the future the climate will stabilize at a new normal, but during the transition everything is uncertain. We don't need to wait for the pronouncement of a climate scientist to know this is true because we are all experiencing it firsthand. Since it is not possible to predict which region of our country or which part of the world will get hammered in any one season, we don't know which food chains will be in jeopardy.

What industrial agriculture has given us is a "just in time" supply system. There are no food reserves to fill grocery shelves when there are shortages. With the COVID-19 pandemic, we have experienced, in a limited fashion, disruptions in beef and pork processing. It could have been far worse. Centralized production, processing, and marketing chains are susceptible to catastrophic failures because industrialized agriculture is predicated on vast acreages of monoculture corn, soybeans, wheat, etc., such that the farmers cannot easily switch to alternative crops.

If the consensus becomes that industrial agriculture should be replaced with a more decentralized, diverse system, the first place to focus is on markets—restoring open competitive markets on the local and regional level. To do that, noncompetitive proprietary market systems for agricultural commodities that operate on a national level will have to be controlled through antitrust enforcement. There is a precedent for this dating from 1921, with the passage of the Packers and Stockyards Act. The consent decree concurrent with the passage of that act required that the five corporations that controlled beef- and pork-packing divested their corporate-owned market places. Henceforth, they were required to purchase hogs and cattle at independent public markets.

The Packers and Stockyards consent decree was effective in an evolutionary rather than revolutionary way, and by the 1970s the US hog and cattle markets were the freest and most competitive ever. The adoption of neoliberal economic policies allowed mergers in pork- and beef-packing, causing a global cartel to develop very quickly. The first priority of the new packing cartel was to marginalize the public open-market system.

Today most of the hogs and cattle these cartels slaughter come through a captive network of growers, often with no pricing determined before the time of delivery. Growers literally accept the terms offered and are given no opportunity to negotiate. If we were to again require that the packers price and purchase fat cattle and hogs in a public forum, this would effectively eliminate the packers' ability to manipulate the market for their own profit. It would, in turn, allow for smaller local firms to bid on an equal basis for their supply.

There was a time when livestock and other commodities were all sold in physical markets. You delivered your crop or livestock to a marketplace and a bid was publicly negotiated. This is no longer necessary, as we now have the internet, which is particularly suited to serve as an inexpensive marketing platform; the market for corn, soybeans, and wheat should no longer need the likes of Cargill, ADM, Bunge, and Dreyfus to act as market intermediaries. There is no reason that the farmer and the ultimate purchaser cannot interface directly through an electronic market. The rest is simply a matter of transportation.

The same is true for livestock. The one market that still functions in the United States in a mostly transparent fashion is that for feeder calves, where both physical auction markets and video/electronic markets function very efficiently. Video/electronic markets for feeder calves are essentially open public markets for contracts for future delivery rather than for the actual physical animal.

The same concept of an open competitive market for future delivery contracts of chickens, pigs, and fat cattle should work very efficiently. That we do not have such markets is because the cartels cannot manipulate and control the system. Take away their ability to exploit the production system and you take away the reason for their dominant size. Local and regional packing plants would have a chance to become established and, with time, transform the entire food production system.

As local and regional markets come into existence, production agriculture can also evolve into smaller, more manageable units, and rural communities would revitalize. But it will take more infrastructure than just farms and marketplaces. For one, we need publicly financed research again. Industrialized agriculture did more than just eliminate public markets; it turned the agricultural scientists working in our university system into hired hands. The seeds, the chemicals, the new generation of robotic machinery, the vaccines, the field studies—they all need to be put back into the public domain.

Access to the retail market also needs to be restored, as retail food stores have merged into just a few global giants. It is more convenient for them to stock their shelves through a small number of large food processors and wholesalers. A local producer of vegetables or jelly or hams may be offering a superior product, but their quantities are too small to interest the likes of Albertsons, Kroger, or Walmart. Somehow, local and regional producers need an efficient mechanism to get their wares in front of the consumers.

A place to start is the next farm bill, where the priority should be—front and center—to revitalize rural America. Antitrust laws need to be dusted off and applied. Diversity in production and marketing on the local and regional levels should become the priority. Supply-management systems need to be restored to better match supply with demand. Trade treaties need to be renegotiated to acknowledge that all countries have the right to food sovereignty—including the United States. These treaties should also ensure that agricultural markets are not subject to manipulation and influence by foreign governments and global corporations. Funding should be restored for public research, and loan programs need to be made available to help beginning farmers and ag-service businesses get reasonably priced financing.

This need to revitalize, or if you will, re-create family farm–based agriculture is important everywhere in America, but it is doubly important in the West. Here the antifarmer policies have had an outsize effect because of the naturally low population densities of the arid lands. Many western towns and cities are now hollow shells, and a number of smaller towns have up and disappeared altogether. The founding influence of the previous form of agriculture that created and shaped this landscape is a distant memory, leaving communities to struggle to maintain cohesion and identity. People are isolated. But wealth is here—enormous wealth. The newly weaned calves and the just-harvested wheat leaves in semitrailer load lots, but when they go, little of that wealth is left behind.

Then we should consider the animosity that has come to dominate the thinking of rural people toward the urban majority. This complicates the creation of a coalition to reform agriculture. Already the Green New Deal is viewed by my neighbors as a socialist plot to eliminate our rural way of life. Mind you, no one has actually read the Green New Deal, but just the fact that it's cosponsored by a young Hispanic woman (Representative Alexandria Ocasio-Cortez) from New York City and has the word "green" in the title is all they need to know. We have come to the point where even our words are incomprehensible to one another, as if we are speaking two different languages.

The perversion of policy has brought us to this junction, and it can only be through deliberate policies that we can restore a vibrant and resilient rural America, one capable of feeding us through the coming uncertainties of climate change.

Normalize from Reality

Musing on the Rural-Urban Political Divide and the Future of Food

In 1968, when I was twenty-two and just out of college, I joined the Peace Corps and, along with a dozen guys of my same age and circumstances, was sent to Somalia to teach farmers the benefits of modern agriculture. We were tasked to promote enhanced production of sorghum, a field crop that, incidentally, had originated in that part of Africa. The main technology that we were to impart was the use of oxen to plow fields, as in that part of Somalia, tillage was done by hand using a short hoe. In truth, the farming practices of the agropastoralists of southern Somalia were, from modern agricultural standards, primitive with low productivity. In their defense, it was low input and not actually labor intensive, with a fairly reliable chance of producing a crop.

Our mission was a total failure. We did not convince one Somali farmer to adopt animal traction. It took me a number of years—including more formal education and much more practical education, both as a rancher and as an agricultural development specialist—to understand why. In the highlands of Ethiopia, not all that far from the fields of southern Somalia, farmers have been using oxen to till their fields for centuries, if not millennia. But the practice did not filter down to the fields bordered by the Shebelle and Jubba Rivers of Somalia for the simple reason that the cattle in southern Somalia were subject to an infection carried by tsetse flies. The skinny, spotted, horned cattle common in that part of Somalia were partially immune to this disease, but because the infection was chronic, they were not robust enough for the serious efforts required to pull a plow.

Following my tour in Somalia, I accidentally fell into another equally fascinating job. I became the aid to Representative Robert Clark Jr., the first African American elected to the Mississippi Legislature since Reconstruction. Needless to say, I learned things that my upbringing in rural Montana had not taught me. It was in Mississippi that I met yet another remarkable man, who had, during the hardest and most dangerous times of the civil rights struggle, helped organize the Black population of the Mississippi Delta to secure the right to vote. It was Henry Lorenzi's conviction that it was the responsibility of the African Americans of Mississippi to take the lead in securing their own civil rights. His role was simply to assist. Henry's academic background was in physics, and he used a laboratory concept about how one should think about effecting change in a complex cultural context. "Normalize from reality" was his succinct advice—a vision on how things can be better is vital, but start with reality.

A little knowledge is a dangerous thing, particularly when it is coupled by a lot of hubris. That, unfortunately, has been the dominant theme in the advice given to African farmers by European and American agricultural experts. But the purpose of this essay is not to discuss this failure in Africa but to explore another failure (a failure also stemming from assumptions and hubris)—the growing political chasm between those who grow food in America and those who consume it. Much of that failure results from the failure to "normalize from reality."

The bulk of modern agriculture produces crops for an industrialized, vertically integrated market system that provides abundant, inexpensive, but not necessarily high-quality food to the consuming public. For more than half a century, farm policy in this country has resulted in putting the smaller family farms out of business, what we in agriculture call the "cheap food policy." The official assertion has been that small farms are inefficient, and the consumer will benefit from less expensive food raised on large farms tied to a global agro-industrial system. The American farmers who have survived the farm policies designed to weed them out individually till more land than ever before possible, using incredibly advanced technology and machines that are impossibly large. But the economics of this industrialized agricultural system keep these farmers in perpetual debt. They are, essentially, "serfs on their own land."

However, the global industrial system of agriculture is subject to all manner of supply chain collapses. For one, our food supply is in jeopardy from the wild swings that we are experiencing in weather, making the production of food increasingly vulnerable. Climatic inconsistency is also exacerbating global income inequality, prompting waves of migration. Regional wars are more frequent, causing countries that previously were somewhat stable to collapse into what we now call "failed states," Syria and Somalia being prime examples. Continued reliance on a food system controlled by global monopolies and cartels is a disaster waiting to happen.

Ironically, however, farmers who are being systematically exploited by big banks and multinational agribusiness hate those whom they identify as environmentalists more than they hate the corporations that keep them in economic thrall. Unless we find a way to bridge this chasm of perceptions, we, as a nation, cannot reach a consensus on how to reestablish an agriculture that is robust, resilient, sustainable, and equitable. If we indeed fail to reach consensus, this country will face a very challenging future.

The Vegetarian Nonsolution

As you can imagine, vegetarians are a perplexing group for people who raise livestock for a living. No one really challenges vegetarianism, as it is a little like religion: if that is what you want to believe, then that is your business. This, however, is not meant to be a polemic against vegetarianism, vegetarians, or vegans but rather an exploration of assumptions that end up dividing rural and urban. The reader might look at this section as a diversion to the scenic route—eventually the roads will merge, and the narrative shall continue in a more direct manner.

So let us explore the main reasons people give for not eating meat. I have heard four main themes: it is an ancient cultural practice, it is more healthful, it is cruel to kill and eat animals, and vegetarianism/veganism is not only better for the environment but also makes food available to the world's hungry. If you grew up in a culture that does not eat meat, your ideas about the proper foods to eat are pretty well fixed. By the same token, if you are a vegetarian out of concern for your health, that is most certainly your own business. However, there are arguments and assumptions made in the advocacy of vegetarianism that are germane to this discussion.

Is it cruel to kill and eat animals? When one invokes the image of Mother Nature, one envisions green meadows, flowers, and butterflies. However, when it comes to protecting the life that Mother Nature so generously provides, she is also callous and indifferent. Nothing living on earth ceases to live except in pain and trauma, and that includes us. We do what we can to protect our final minute from physical or psychic pain but rarely succeed.

Mother Nature is lavish with life. Thousands of baby turtles hatch on a beach; lusting for survival, they make a mad dash for the sea, but only hundreds make it to the surf, where they face a whole new array of predators. Out of that whole hatch, only a handful ever make it to maturity to return to that beach and lay eggs for the next orgy of death. The mammals have it no better. On the Serengeti Plain, no wildebeest ever dies of a peaceful old age, and the predatory lions have their own troubles. A wound from a cape buffalo's horn festers, and that lion can no longer keep up with the pride. She dies, lying under a thorn tree from dehydration and starvation. Every lion, unless killed outright, ultimately dies of starvation.

So, does not killing a cow, butchering it, and then cooking its flesh over a barbecue somehow protect that cow from not dying a violent death? I don't think so. One could counter and say that if that cow was not born in the first place, then it would not be alive to be killed in a gigantic factory designed to disassemble hundreds of cows per hour.

But one needs to consider what we learned from Charles Darwin. One of his insights was that if a food source exists, some kind of living organism will adapt to exploit it. If that cow, described in the paragraph above, was not born on the plains of Montana to consume grass, something else would be born and consume that grass. Maybe small things like rodents and rabbits, maybe larger animals like deer, elk, and buffalo. But each one of those lives, great or small, would only survive by constant vigilance against predators. And if they somehow survive the predators and also survive drought, fire, and winter, at the end of their natural lives, they will die from infirmity and starvation.

In the scheme of things, not killing and eating that cow has not protected anything from violence and trauma. What is more moral—the death of one cow or the death of three hundred rabbits? Is a big life more important than a small life or a number of small lives? There's no real answer to that one, although I suspect that a mouse is just as traumatized at its demise in the jaws of a cat as an elephant at the wrong end of a poacher's bullet.

We can all look back two hundred thousand years to our common mother. If she, her mate, and their children had not evolved the ability to run down and spear their prey, none of us would be here today. Ultimately, we are that predator species. No matter how sanitized we have made the process of raising, killing, and processing animals—so that, as a consumer, we can purchase a pretty package and be completely divorced from the savagery that Mother Nature initially devised—we are still a predator.

That does not mean that cruelty does not matter. It is neither ethical nor good animal husbandry to be cruel to animals. Animal rights advocates, often over the top in what they consider to be animal cruelty, are correct in their efforts to give more space and better living conditions to chickens, hogs, and veal calves in the factory farms where they are raised in today's industrialized agricultural system.

The next question is whether vegetarianism/veganism is better for the environment and allows for more food to be available to feed the world's hungry? The argument is made by some vegetarians, and others, that it takes a number of pounds of corn (better known as maize in the rest of the world) to produce a pound of chicken, pork, or beef. Cattle are the least efficient in converting corn to beef. Therefore, if that corn were not fed to livestock, it could feed the world's hungry.

In theory, it could, but the main cause of hunger is political and economic. There is currently enough food in the world; it is the distribution and access to that food that is the constraint. According to a 2019 report by the Food and Agriculture Organization of the United Nations, food insecurity affects 2 billion of the world's population (25.9 percent). Among those are 690 million people who are chronically undernourished.[1]

So we have an anomaly. Farmers in America and the rest of the world are going broke because they raise a surplus of corn and soybeans, while two billion of the world's population is hungry. A big reason that there is enough food in the world is the geographical accident that is Iowa, which has the perfect climate and soil to grow corn and soybeans in rotation. Farmers in Iowa, and the states adjoining Iowa, grow so much corn and soybeans that it cannot all be sold. It creates a worldwide surplus.

This is why US farm policy, for the entire last half of the twentieth century, discouraged farmers from raising corn. At times, farmers were paid not to plant but just keep their fields fallow. Now in the twenty-first century, that problem has been temporarily solved by turning corn into ethanol to fuel our cars. There is an ongoing debate about whether ethanol is actually as environmentally friendly as claimed. Whether it is or not, the key reason we convert a sizable portion of each year's corn crop to ethanol is economic, not environmental. Without that annual diversion, corn prices would collapse, which, in turn, would collapse the prices for every other crop that farmers raise. The resulting economic depression would be felt worldwide.

Raising chickens, pigs, and cattle and feeding them "surplus" grains and kitchen scraps has a long history that almost certainly dates to when people first started settled agriculture in Mesopotamia. In more modern times, it is a practice by which farm families could market cream, eggs, chickens, or pigs for cash with which to buy necessities, such as new shoes for the children at the beginning of winter.

But in Iowa, following World War II, an abundance of corn resulted in prices less than the cost of planting, raising, and harvesting it. Iowa farmers began to calculate that if they fed their corn to pigs or beef cattle, they could possibly net a profit rather than a certain loss. You might wonder, if raising corn was unprofitable, why did farmers plant corn in the first place? The reason is that the cost of buying the land is a fixed cost. Planting a crop at a net loss is still less of a financial loss than not planting at all, or, for that matter, planting something else that would not yield as much as corn and, therefore, result in a lower overall gross income. So in the fall after harvest, a farmer would calculate the probable market price for the corn and decide whether buying a bunch of weaner pigs or young calves and feeding them out was a better bet than selling the corn outright.

It was not long before agribusiness corporations saw what farmers were doing and decided that they, too, could cash in. From this beginning developed the factory chicken and hog systems and the cattle feedlots that raise hundreds of thousands of steers at a time. Now we have chickens, pigs, and cattle genetically selected to work in this industrial animal-raising system. But the entire system would fall apart if the price of corn and soybeans rises too high. Therefore, the agribusiness corporations, in cahoots with the big banks, carefully control farm policy to guarantee that corn and soybeans never become actually profitable. It is a moneymaking scheme that extracts profits for global corporations and big banks by keeping farmers in perpetual debt. That was a long-winded way of saying that choosing to not eat chicken, pork, or beef does not help feed the world's poor or somehow benefit the environment. In one sense, the factory farming system is highly efficient—chicken, pork, and beef is, relative to the actual costs of raising, very cheap. Inexpensive enough that you will find chicken rotisseries on many Third World city streets. Roast chicken is available to world's less poor, if not the world's poorest of the poor.

It is true that the world's population is continuing to grow, and uncertainty has been injected into our food production systems by climatic instability. There will probably come a time when the price of corn will be higher than the cost of feeding it to livestock. When that time comes, the amount of animal protein available on the market will decrease, and the price for fried chicken or a hamburger will be higher than what the masses can afford. When that time comes, vegetarianism will no longer be just a lifestyle choice.

Biodiversity and Agriculture

Somehow in the decades since I graduated from college, the concept of biodiversity has come to dominate thinking about biological and natural systems. This term has seemingly entered the popular consciousness as a dogma, religious in nature—an end in and to itself. In the minds of some people, all problems or deficiencies that we detect in nature is the result of insufficient biodiversity and can be remedied by increasing that diversity. But little consideration is given to the contradictions. The biggest, the one that is right there like the nose on your face, is agriculture. The whole point of agriculture is to minimize biodiversity in order to maximize productivity.

Ten thousand years ago, before human beings began to alter the world through agriculture and herding, biodiversity was what happened; it was the only system, and Mother Nature was ruthlessly in charge. But the number of people in the world very slowly began to multiply until suddenly we had an explosion of human beings. Maybe some want to deny the facts, but realistically, how could eight billion human beings *not* significantly affect the natural world and the world's weather patterns? And in so doing, the diversity of nature is increasingly being compromised.

This domination by human beings might be lamentable to one's notions of the natural world, but it is the reality with which we must live. Mother Nature's method of regulation is not benign. There is no equilibrium that balances the natural system. It is, instead, an endless series of boom and bust. Good weather and good rains result in lush pastures. Life that consumes vegetation proliferates. Life that preys on that vegetarian life, in turn, increases. Rains fail, winter is unrelenting, animals die—first the consumers of vegetation, followed by the predators. The next year, or the next decade, or even after scores of decades, good weather and good rains result again in lush pastures, and the cycle recommences.

Animals have adapted to the booms and the inevitable collapses as best they can. Some develop patterns of migration, others habits of hibernation. But no matter how resilient they become, they still cannot beat the system. But we human beings have elected to try to control Mother Nature herself. The point of agriculture is to minimize the effects of the climatic fluctuations. Plant varieties are carefully selected to maximize production in the specific microclimate that one is attempting to cultivate. Livestock are chosen and carefully managed to provide maximum production, given the environment available to the herder. Farmers wage a continuous battle against weeds, insects, and pathogens. Herders guard against predators and vaccinate against diseases.

Does that mean that biodiversity has no place in agriculture? Not at all. Soils contain a complex mixture of micro- and larger organisms. We have limited scientific understanding of their roles and interactions, but it is important in soil fertility. Pastures and hayfields benefit from a mixture of grasses that respond differently to climatic fluctuations. Cool, wet springs favor certain plants, while in warm, drier springs, other grasses dominate. However, there are other plants—such as introduced invaders or hardy native plants with little nutritional value or that may even be poisonous—that we don't want. It depends—diversity has its place and its limits.

But biodiversity is often used to justify everyone's notion of land management. For instance, a recent news article in *Deseret News* featured a Utah man concerned about the lack of rejuvenation of aspen groves caused in his estimation by excessive numbers of deer and elk.[2] His solution is more wolves and mountain lions. No doubt that would work, but at what cost and to whom? The fact that wolves and mountain lions would also be killing livestock did not seem to even factor in his mission to protect trees.

There is a very different mind-set between people who see themselves as environmentalists and/or conservationists and those who practice agriculture. The environmental/conservation perspective is from the external looking inward toward the particular. The agricultural point of observation is from the particular looking outward. It is the same landscape that is being considered, but what each one sees as important is very different. From a farmer/herder point of view, what is important is a very specific, often generational, detailed knowledge of the land that is under the farmer's care. What are its limitations and how can that particular piece of land be coaxed to provide maximum productivity?

An environmentalist's or conservationist's motivation might be more varied. Depending on the person's particular inclinations, they can be concerned about specific plant or animal species, overall soil health, watershed protection, or recreational potential. It is the bigger picture that is more important than the details.

Modern technological, industrialized agriculture has incrementally increased plant and animal productivity. Each crop, each animal species raised, rests on an incredible body of cultural, practical, and scientific knowledge. Each crop, each animal species raised, is produced under a complex economic system that requires specific timely inputs. The resulting product is sold into markets that aggregate, transform, and ultimately distribute those products to the consuming public.

Modern farmers are not technological idiots. It takes both a good education and a lot of practical experience to bring in a crop and still survive economically to plant again in the coming spring. But farming and herding have never been the occupations of technological idiots, no matter what one read as a child about the country mouse and his cousin, the sophisticated city mouse. To survive from year to year always required careful observation and a willingness to learn. A multigenerational knowledge of the land, its capability, and limitations is helpful.

While modern technological, industrialized agriculture has succeeded in providing abundant harvests and the supermarket shelves overflow with a dizzying variety of food choices, there is a dark side. A handful of chain oligopolies controls inputs and outputs for all major crops, along with the essential decision-making. The government and the banks enforce the rules of industrial agriculture. It is a top-down system that works only because it allows farmers the illusion of independence. Farmers' culture and work ethic motivate them to exploit their own and their families' labor. The market system for agricultural commodities has been systematically subverted to the point that there is no longer any transparency or competition. Prices are simply determined at the top, and the producer accepts what is offered.

But vast monocultures of corn, soybeans, and wheat and huge factory-size barns full of chickens, pigs, and milk cows are vulnerable to adverse climatic fluctuations and introduced pathogens. The more the genetics of a crop in a given locality is identical, the more vulnerable it becomes. There is a kind of inverse relationship between plants and animals that have been selected for high productivity and the ability of that highly productive variety to be able to resist adverse conditions. Modern agriculture is dependent on providing perfect growing conditions to maximize yields. Less-than-perfect conditions can lead to very poor results.

Different genetic traits can be bred in to make a plant resistant to drought or to a specific pathogen, but geneticists cannot select for a large number of resistance factors at one time because that negatively affects maximum productivity. Therefore, you can't stack in a whole lot of genetic resistance traits, just in case something bad happens. It is, therefore, vitally important to have access to a diverse pool of genetic traits from which agricultural scientists can breed varieties resistant to any emerging threat. Another point where biodiversity is critically important.

Because global warming is increasing the incidence of bad weather, and globalism is spreading diseases and disease vectors around the world faster than authorities can respond, we may very well be approaching the time for a reckoning. This industrialized system of agriculture, like so many of the industries on which modern society relies, is complex, interconnected, and brittle. In agriculture, this is compounded by a market that no longer signals to the farmer what is the best course of action. Centralized management of any large complex system works well while it works. When it fails, it can fail catastrophically.

The Trouble with Conservationists/ Environmentalists

Conservationists and/or environmentalists have been somewhat dismissive of the role played in the environment by farmers and ranchers. You might even say careless or cavalier. The conservation movement covers a wide range of issues, and often the one hand does not know or agree with what the other is saying. Issues range from those that are vitally important to the future of humanity to those that are driven by pure fantasy.

In this discussion, I will mostly limit myself to conservation issues that are being fought in Montana. The citizens of Montana have had knock-down, drag-out fights over just about everything rural, including mineral extraction, land use policy, and wildlife.

Mineral Extraction

The mineral extraction issues include hard-rock mining, coal strip-mining, coalbed methane, and oil drilling with fracking. These are important industries, central to our economy. But mineral extraction also comes with a long history that considers the land and the local population, the neighbors you might say, expendable for the greater good of society and the shareholders—particularly the shareholders.

When the impacted population of mineral extraction are farmers and ranchers who own the land surrounding a coal strip mine in southeastern Montana, they can easily be just rolled over. In fact, the law allows this, because the laws were written by the mineral extraction industry. Strangely, or you might say ironically, Montana was a world-class mining economy before it became a frontier. Gold was discovered and mined as of 1864, before Montana was even minimally settled by Euro-Americans. Montana's mining millionaires helped write the 1872 mining law that gave preference to the mineral extraction industry over all other users of the land. To this day, that law continues to give mining and oil exploration priority.

In Montana, fighting for the protection of the land and the rights of the neighbors of mineral extraction sites has seen some bitter battles. Generally, the extraction industry has gotten its way, in the process making billions of dollars. But resistance has resulted in some improvements to air and water quality and reclamation regulations. To get this done, the farmers and ranchers needed assistance from environmentalists.

The era of fossil fuel extraction has almost run its course. Coal is no longer a preferred or even an economic fuel. Oil is in surplus. Only gas is still needed to energize our economy. The fight continues to require that the strip mines that are now going out of production are reclaimed as the law requires. But bankruptcy is a good (and legal) way for the mineral extraction companies to avoid the costs of reclamation. As I mentioned above, the mining interests wrote the laws.

But who gets blamed for the closure of gold mines, strip mines, and oil drilling? The conservationist even when the conservationist is a fellow farmer or rancher. In Montana, it has been farmers and ranchers who have had a prominent role in the fight for more environmentally responsible mineral extraction. The controversy is that along with the bad parts of mineral extraction come the jobs. And often it is the children of rural Montanans who have those jobs. In the small towns, you can sense the love/hate over mineral extraction. People know that some of what was being done to the environment and to the neighbors was wrong, but without those jobs, their children would be long gone.

I bring up these issues because it is wrong for environmentalists to assume that farmers and ranchers are automatically opposed to everything that may be proposed to protect the environment. People who make a living from the land are, for the most part, passionate about protecting their land. If encouraged to speak, they may prove to be more sympathetic than many might suppose. Farmers and ranchers may even have something important to contribute. However, in this era of hyperpolitical partisanship, we can be having a knock-down, drag-out fight without fighting over the same thing. The people pulling the political strings are very adept at framing arguments to elicit vehement responses. This is how they keep control and continue to make money.

Land Use

Montana is the fourth-largest state, with 37.5 percent in public lands, including national parks, wilderness areas, wildlife refuges, national monuments, national and state forests, and public rangelands.[3] All of them come with conflicting notions as to how they should be managed and for whose benefit. I will focus on two: forests and rangelands.

Montana was part and parcel of the controversy that raged through the 1980s about saving the old-growth forests, wildlife habitat, and the unsightliness of clear-cut timber harvesting. An entire edifice of righteousness on the part of conservationists formed around the movement to preserve the forests. And in their hubris, they succeeded. The lumber mills shut down, and the loggers now use their chainsaws to make wooden bears to sell to tourists.

We are reaping the rewards of policy that was based on insufficient science and hyperventilated righteousness. For a number of years in a row, wildfires have ravaged California, even burning whole cities to the ground. The fires also burn in Oregon and Washington. Montana, at least for this past year, was somewhat spared. For those who live downwind, as I do, the fires that have destroyed the lives of thousands of people, have also looked, smelled, and felt like air pollution, not to mention all of the greenhouse gases released into the atmosphere.

Conservationists proved to be no better than the timber companies and the Forest Service in managing a very complex ecosystem that includes humans as well as trees. I am being somewhat unfair, because one cannot blame conservationists for the entirety of the problem. What we have witnessed and are living through is the collision of two polarized mind-sets occupying the same landscape. You have the libertarian notion that rejects land use planning—I will do what I want, build where I like, and live in the middle of the forest if I take the notion. Then you have those who believe that the forests and mountains can be put under a bell jar and kept as untouched and pristine as they imagine them to have been through eternity.

What I read and what I hear on the radio and TV about how to control the devastation caused by massive fires is confusing. This may be because the experts also do not know what to do. The ecology of the forests and the requirements of the people who live within the forests are too complex for any pat answers. Certainly, locking out the timber companies was not a solution—not to mention the hypocrisy of it all. The lumber needed for the housing boom of recent decades came from somewhere. If the two-by-four did not come from the forests of the American West, it came from Canada or Indonesia instead.

I heard recently on the radio a forest manager talking enthusiastically about prescribed burns. In my estimation, he was being unrealistically naïve. Controlling a planned fire is tough, because things can easily get out of hand. For instance, the planned burn in New Mexico set by the Forest Service in 2022 burned over five hundred square miles and displaced thousands of people. The liability from that one incident runs in the billions of dollars.[4] Where forest managers can, they probably can have limited prescribed fires, particularly where lack of grazing or other forms of control have resulted in the accumulation of undesirable species of shrubs and trees. However, in all probability, because of liability issues, prescribed fires will never be used on a scale large enough to the solve the problem of excess fuel. At best, it is a solution for small situations to protect homes.

We also hear the argument that if we let small wildfires burn instead of stamping them out, there would be less fuel and therefore less intense fires. That has some common sense, especially in terrain that is impossible to access with ground crews and equipment. However, risking fires that get out of control does not seem like a sensible way to deal with the forests where people live in scattered communities and homesteads, particularly where drought and high winds increase the risk of massive wildfires.

The return of logging is probably a more important intervention and least harmful to everyone. Grazing is not often mentioned, but part of the movement to preserve the forests in their supposably primeval splendor was to eliminate grazing by domestic livestock. Much of the overload of fuel in the mountains is grass and shrubs. Grazing by cattle, sheep, and goats was and can be again an important management tool. Grazing by wild animals is not adequate because there are not enough of them concentrated in the right places during the right times of the year to consume the excess vegetation. Finally, zoning and regulations regarding where people can live and what they can build are inevitable.

When it come to the rangelands, the issues are much more germane to my personal situation. To my immediate south, a pair of billionaire brothers have purchased two hundred thousand acres and use the land as a private hunting reserve. It reminds me of the trip my wife and I took to central France to visit a region where, in the beginning of the sixteenth century, the French king enclosed a private hunting reserve for himself. Right in the middle, he built Chambord, a magnificent palace just for his hunting trips. Look it up: it is a beautiful example of French renaissance architecture, and Leonardo da Vinci was involved in its design.

The billionaire brothers have created their own royal hunting preserve. Each has a hotel-size mansion, but they share a private runway for their private airliner. Their comings and goings are hidden by security staff. On their private hunting reserve, they keep 7,400 of the public's elk just for their own pleasure.

The problem is that this elk population is ten times greater than what the Montana Fish, Wildlife, and Parks department considers optimum for the hunting district. During the hunting season, the public is not allowed access to the public's elk, because the land is private. After the hunting season closes, the elk disperse onto all of the neighbors' property, mine included, where they live the rest of the year from grass and hay we depend on to feed our livestock.

I have no idea if the billionaire brothers consider themselves conservationists. Perhaps they do. However, being a neighbor is obviously not important to them. They do nothing for and contribute little to the community, but their elk certainly harms us. It is a modern-day version of out-of-touch aristocracy, much like the French kings at Chambord.

North of me there is another version of colonialism. The American Prairie Reserve (APR) is purchasing ranches along both banks of the Missouri River with the plan to link them through the adjoining public land into a two-hundred-by-one-hundred-mile block (3.1 million acres) for wild bison. To keep the bison population in check and on the move, they propose more predators, particularly wolves and grizzly bears.

Needless to say, this vision has alarmed the local ranching community, myself included. So far, the response remains alarm, not arms, but given the anger, that could very well change. The premise from the APR perspective is that ranching in this semiarid landscape has harmed the natural vegetative flora, along with the small fauna that are dependent on the short-grass prairie.

According to the APR literature, my neighbors and I are despoiling the natural environment, and it requires outside expertise, backed by funding from a handful of globe-trotting billionaires, to save us from ourselves. In the APR vision, a large herd of free-roaming bison, harried by wolves and grizzly bears, will—through natural grazing pressure—restore the prairie to its pristine condition. By restoring the prairie, the sparrows and other small creatures will return and thrive.

The APR does not offer proof that any of this is true, but serious money is being donated to see the project to its fruition. This concept, called by some "rewilding," is strong in Great Britain, where a similar large-scale project is proposed in Scotland, funded by some of the same billionaires who donate to the APR. The narrative over there is that sheep and deer have altered the environment of Scotland to the extent that they must be removed from the landscape in order to restore it to what it once was.

In October 2020, the *Economist* ran an article "In Their Sights" that elicited this response from Robyn Boere, associate lecturer in Christian ethics at the University of St. Andrews, and Neil Stange, a professional agrologist:

> This concept of natural excludes humans, but at the same time envisages a highly managed human-constructed landscape achieved by human processes, undertaken for human goals, and based on the best human guesses of what those landscapes used to be. . . . But let us call rewilding what it is: another attempt to manage our natural environment for specifically human goals. It should thus be morally evaluated and debated like all other human projects and goals.
> . . . It is this and not some mystical prehuman status, that makes it properly natural.[5]

These examples outlined above form the reality faced by farmers and ranchers striving to stay economically viable yet independent from corporate control. I have outlined my personal concerns, but farmers and ranchers all over this nation have their own similar issues to deal with. Our lives, our work, our knowledge, our culture, and our communities are often not considered important or respected by those who have alternative visions of how our land should be managed.

Conflicts over Wildlife, Recreation, and Agriculture

A few years back, I had the opportunity to watch elephants coming to water at the springs in Kenya's Amboseli National Park at the foot of Mount Kilimanjaro. We were sitting in our Land Rover, watching a group of twenty or so elephants approach the springs. At first, it looked as though the big bull, a truly huge and magnificent animal, was carrying a stick in his trunk. But when he got close, we saw that it was a spear that pierced his trunk. It was obviously painful.

We informed the rangers that one of their elephants was wounded. Presumably, they tranquilized the beast, removed the spear, and administered a huge dose of antibiotics. At least, that is what I like to believe happened. However, I got to wondering about the rest of the story. How did the spear get in the elephant's trunk? What motivated someone to stand in front of a bull elephant and fling a spear at it? Did that person even survive the encounter?

My presumption is that this elephant was raiding some poor farmer's field, and he was defending his crop the only way available to him. The interface between wildlife and agriculture is getting more and more complicated, and an elephant or two in your corn patch is a huge problem when that is all there is to feed your family.

On TV nature shows, we see how elephants are being slaughtered by poachers for their ivory. There is a fierce worldwide debate about whether any ivory at all should be legally sold, even from places acknowledged to have a surplus of elephants. And, of course, there are appeals for donations to save the elephants. But somehow, the farmer who has to coexist with the elephant gets little consideration, either on TV or in the debate on how to save elephants, and the farmers certainly receive little of the money sent for the elephants' benefit.

I did not have to go so far afield for an example of the interface between wildlife, their defenders, and those who make a living through agriculture. My home state of Montana abounds with those conflicts and controversies. Grizzly bears have become a frightening reality for ranch families living in the northern Rocky Mountains. Many parents dare not let their children play outdoors and do not venture about in their work without arming themselves.

Every wild animal appears to have its own army of partisans. Coyotes, eagles, wolves, grizzly bears, and ferrets among the predator species; bison, feral horses, elk, deer, antelope, prairie dogs, turkeys, sage hens, and desert tortoise among the grass eaters—all have their own band of crusaders, complete with armor, lances, and a battle flag flying an image of their favored animal superimposed on a holy red cross. And just like that Kenyan spear-chucking farmer, America's farmers and ranchers are expected to welcome and feed these animals. And when we object, it is the farmers and ranchers who are the perceived villains.

The entire drama of the Bundy family protests in Nevada and Oregon, and the ultimate gunning down of one of their supporters by federal agents, was triggered by the BLM reducing the Bundys' grazing allotment, claiming cattle interfered with the desert tortoise. My brother in Arkansas has a new neighbor, from who knows where, that calls the sheriff every time he moves his cattle on the county road that passes through her property. It all adds up to a sense of us versus them.

The issue is compounded, both in Africa and in Montana, by the lack of land tenure. In Kenya, the state owns much of the land in the name of the people. Some parcels near cities and valuable farm ground are privately registered, but often land adjacent to national parks is open to customary tribal usage. This means that the farmers and herders have no permanent legal right to use that land and, therefore, no incentive to construct wildlife-proof fences, even if they could afford to do so.

In Montana, 37.5 percent of the land is owned by either the federal government or the state. Except for the land designated as national parks, wildlife refuges, and wilderness, that land has historically been managed for logging, mining, oil extraction, hunting, and grazing. The conflict comes when wildlife and recreational advocates desire to change the designation to exclude logging, mining, oil wells, and in particular grazing by livestock, in order to make more room for their favorite wild animal. Since it is government land, i.e., public land, and a portion of the public, namely themselves, feels passionately that wolves, for instance, are needed for a healthy environment, the privately owned cows should be required to go. This, of course, does not make the rancher with a lease to graze public lands happy. If the wolves would stay on the public land, perhaps an accommodation could be made, but wolves, like elephants, don't respect boundaries.

And here is the crux of the resentment felt by many rural residents against the urban "environmentalists." Farmers and ranchers, like most any of us, don't clearly understand the intricacies of macroeconomic policy and global markets in which we all participate and in which they, as farmers, must sell the harvest. Like the weather, the political/economic system is something to worry about, and one does what one can to protect oneself, but it will rain or it will not rain. It is out of our hands. Likewise, prices will be good or they will be bad, and that, too, is out of our hands.

However, wolves or grizzly bears killing calves is personal. Being informed that this is natural and that biodiversity is a sign of a healthy ecosystem is insulting and an existential threat—like being mugged. Sure, it is money right out of your pocket, but it is more. Your personal space has been violated. It is disrespect and an insult to what a farmer or rancher is most proud of. Remember, those concerned from an environmental perspective are looking from the general toward the particular, but farmers and ranchers are most concerned about this acre right here under their feet. It is their inheritance, the place on the earth where they have been put in charge. It is their personal responsibility to protect that piece of land and make it as productive as possible. It is not surprising that a farmer might resent interference in their domain, with other people telling them, who have lived here all their life, what to do on their own land.

Coyotes and Wolves

Before the attention of conservationists turned to wolves, a faction of the wildlife advocates focused on protecting coyotes, which livestock raisers had been attempting to control ever since cattle and sheep were introduced to the West. The campaign to protect coyotes ramped up in the early 1970s, but coyotes then and now have no trouble looking after themselves. They are highly adaptable, making themselves at home everywhere in North America, even in the big cities. The coyote aficionados, however, were not constrained to the truth in their advocacy to prevent lethal methods of coyote control. In the early 1970s, I heard someone on TV declaring that there is no evidence that coyotes had ever killed a lamb. That is an assertion that any number of shepherds, myself included, can attest to be a complete fabrication, as we have witnessed coyotes killing sheep.

When you have a flock of sheep and are losing up to 20 percent of the lambs to coyotes, the effect is demoralizing. When I was young, almost all of the ranches in this part of central Montana had sheep; now I am the last holdout. Coyote predation was not the only reason for ranchers to get out of the sheep business, but it was the most important.

The coyote advocates were only partially successful in restricting coyote control. Their main win was in banning government predator-control agents from using poison baits. More significant was a worldwide movement opposing fur coats. The fashion industry turned against natural fur to such an extent that trappers had a hard time making a living. This antifur fad has since run its course, and coyotes are again being hunted, trapped, and worn, but a lot of harm was done to ranchers, hunters, and trappers for no good reason.

At some point, attention turned from coyotes to wolves. It took a couple of decades of escalating pressure and false narratives to get it done, but wolves were transplanted to Yellowstone National Park in 1995. Along the way, we were told that no one should be afraid of wolves, because there was no evidence, ever, that wolves attacked people. This, of course, is a lie—wolves were a definite danger on the frontier. The public was fed a line, disguised as a scientific law, that only with wolves could Yellowstone be natural and sustainable. Wolves, we were told, were the magic ingredient needed to naturally manage the herds of elk and bison. In the absence of wolves, Yellowstone simply would not be complete and tourists would be disappointed.

In the opinion of Montana's ranchers, the wolves had been shot and trapped out in the 1930s, and good riddance. There is little middle ground. The wolf advocates prevailed because the National Park Service came to see wolves as a potential star attraction. Go to the park and the literature they hand you at the entrance features wolves, just as at Disney World, where Mickey and Minnie grace the cover.

From that first little group of transplanted wolves, the numbers have increased and they have migrated in every direction outside the park. In Montana, the wildlife services admit to there being 833 wolves (not including those in Yellowstone). It should be noted that not all of these wolves derive from the introduced wolves, as there were scattered packs all over western Montana. The wolf recovery goals were met in 2002, but it wasn't until 2011 that wolves were actually delisted from endangered status and became subject to management.[6] Up until then, it was a federal crime to shoot a wolf, even if it was in the act of killing your livestock. That period between 2002 and 2011 was taken up by court cases brought by wolf advocacy groups to prevent the control and management of wolves, even though the agreed-upon wolf recovery goals had already been met and exceeded.

The 833 wolves now officially residing in Montana require a lot of maintenance. Verified livestock losses in 2019 by wolf predation were 46 cattle, 20 sheep, and 2 horses. In addition, there were 9 cattle and 1 sheep that were probable but unconfirmed kills by wolves. However, this is only 50 percent of what ranchers reported; the other half could not be confirmed.[7] In addition to those that cannot be confirmed, there are livestock that just disappeared. When the herds are brought down from summer pasture with a short count, it is often impossible to find the remains in rugged terrain. In the hot summer of Montana, a carcass can, in just a couple of days, be reduced to nothing but scattered bones by predators, scavengers, and maggots. Unless you happen to ride very near the remains, they are easy to miss. Even the odor dissipates within a week.

Some might say that the loss of 46 cattle, or even twice or four times that number, may seem like a small price to pay for the presence of wolves in the environment. That is like saying to someone in New York City that it is no big deal if you are mugged for the cash in your pockets. So what? You have more, and the person who mugged you needed the money. True, there is a program to compensate livestock owners for lost animals, but the loss must be verified and only pays an average market value for the animal. There is no compensation for the missing livestock or for the work spent trying to prevent predation.

It is all a matter of perspective and what you might consider important. For livestock producers, it is not just a matter of direct losses, because it requires extra work to prevent predation. Guard dogs can help, but they are expensive and feeding them is a costly daily chore. Frequent riding to monitor the situation in remote pastures takes time from other important work. Building special fences is expensive and not that useful. The plain fact is that raising livestock in the presence of major predators is expensive, difficult, and a plain pain in the neck.

Because of confirmed predation, 72 wolves were killed by predator-control agents in 2019. Another 298 were taken by hunters and trappers.[8] This means that every year, 44 percent of the wolves in Montana must be legally culled in order for wolf numbers to stay stable. But no one who ranches or hunts believes that there are only 833 wolves in Montana; there are too many anecdotal sightings in places where wolves are not officially acknowledged to exist. That those sightings never become official might mean that the viewer was mistaken or that someone took care of the problem. If the latter is the case, it points to a serious rift between the advocates for wolves and the people who live with the reality of the wolves.

This brings us back to the wolves of Yellowstone. The park is almost all in Wyoming, so the statistics mentioned above do not include the situation in Yellowstone itself. Apparently, as of 2023 there are 108 wolves in the park.[9] That is a very small number considering the size of the park and the abundance of potential prey. At the time of wolf reintroduction, it was presented as a scientific fact that predators are required to keep populations of prey in check and overall health.

We were informed that wolves were required to keep the herds of elk and bison in balance by culling the old and the weak. That, of course, is not at all true. Any old sheepherder can vouch that predators kill the young and succulent and ignore the old and lame. If anything, it is the availability of prey that determines the abundance of predators, not the other way around. Nature, short of management by man, is subject to wild pendulum swings from overpopulation to underpopulation. Drought and its opposite, along with disease, are what ultimately determine the numbers of predators and prey. Nature is never static; it is always in transition between excess and insufficiency. Rainfall controls the growth of grass, which, in turn, controls the numbers of herbivores, which ultimately controls the number of predators.

It is, therefore, not the predators that keep herds of prey in balance, because for nature, there is no balance. For us, with our short life-spans, it may look like a balance, and there are landscapes we find indescribably wonderful, landscapes we want to preserve forever just as is, and should preserve to the best of our abilities, including the wildlife that so fascinate us. The mix of prey and predators is a tool in that mission to preserve, but we should not confuse the tools with the mission.

In respect to the elk population, wolves seem to have contributed to a decrease in numbers. At the time of wolf introductions in the mid-1990s, there were about 13,000 elk in the park. As of 2020, there are about 6,000.[10] The way that elk calve makes them vulnerable to losing the young to predators. Elk calving season is spread out over a three-month period when the cows disperse to have privacy. This makes their young vulnerable to predators.

Moose, too, have been on the decline. There used to be about 1,000 in Yellowstone, and estimates are that there are currently only 200.[11] Bison numbers do not seem to be particularly affected by wolves. In 2023, there are around 5,900, exceeding the target number by 2,900 head. Each winter, the State of Montana, along with the National Park Service, captures and culls between 600 and 1,000 to keep the bison numbers from becoming excessive for the available feed.[12] Without culling, the bison would migrate farther into Montana onto private land or starve during the next severe winter. Most of the captured bison are transported to a slaughter facility for the benefit of Montana's Indian tribes. The tribes are also allowed to hunt (harvest) a number directly. A small number of bison are quarantined to ensure that they are disease free before they, too, are donated to one of the tribes to augment herds on the reservations.

Bison

The issue of excess bison exiting Yellowstone is another area of conflict between ranchers and wildlife enthusiasts. The park's bison have a high incidence of the disease brucellosis, which induces abortion in cattle and undulant fever in humans. In 1934, the federal government and state governments cooperated on a campaign to eliminate brucellosis in the United States. That campaign has been almost completely successful, except that the last reservoir of brucellosis in the nation are in the park's bison and elk. For this reason, there are strict controls on bison exiting the park to ensure that they do not intermingle with cattle. The reason for culling bison is twofold: to prevent overgrazing within the park, and to keep bison numbers at a level where they do not have to exit the park for their winter survival, in which case they would risk passing brucellosis to cattle.

A cadre of activists has formed to oppose every aspect of controls on Yellowstone's bison, and they do not hesitate from fabricating their own set of facts. Perhaps it is best to let the Buffalo Field Campaign speak for itself. The following is taken from their website:

> Cattle grazing in Montana makes up less than one-quarter of 1 percent of total U.S. beef production. Because it takes seventy-three times the land base to raise a cow in Montana as it does in Iowa, and because a cow in the West requires fifty acres of grazing land for every one acre required in the East, millions of acres of public land are now overgrazed to the point where they can no longer support native flora and fauna.
>
> Despite the unsuitability of much of Montana for raising cattle, livestock producers wield tremendous power. Using the false claim that wild bison could transmit the livestock disease brucellosis to cattle—something that has never occurred—the State of Montana sued the federal government for "allowing" wild bison to migrate out of Yellowstone National Park. After years of legal wrangling, the judge ordered both sides to negotiate their differences and work together on a management plan for wild bison. The Interagency Bison Management Plan (IBMP), signed into effect in December of 2000, was the result. The Plan's stated purpose, "to maintain a wild, free ranging population of bison and address the [scientifically non-existent] risk of brucellosis transmission to protect the economic interest and viability of the livestock industry in the state of Montana" set the stage for the largest bison slaughter since the 19th century.

This statement includes a number of either deliberate or ignorant falsehoods. The first is the assertion that Montana is a marginal place for cattle raising. Just as the climate and forage in Montana is ideal for bison, it is also perfect for cattle. Bison and cattle are, after all, very closely related and can interbreed. In fact, Montana numbers among the most ideal places in the world to raise cattle.

Public lands are also not overgrazed in Montana. You do not have to take my word for this; the BLM regularly publishes reports on the condition of the rangelands.[13] Ironically, the worst example of overgrazing on public lands that I have witnessed is in Yellowstone

National Park, where sagebrush dominates pastures that should be grass and where little brushy vegetation exists along the banks of the Lamar and Yellowstone Rivers. You don't have to be a range expert to see the difference. Just drive from Livingston, Montana, up the Paradise Valley and into the park's northern entrance at Gardiner, and the overgrazing is immediately apparent.

The assertion that bison have never transmitted brucellosis to cattle is true in recent years only because the park's bison are not allowed to comingle with cattle because of the Interagency Bison Management Plan. In fact, the reverse is true. Brucellosis is an "old world" disease that was introduced to bison by cattle.[14] The Spaniards in the Southwest mixed cattle with wild bison as early as the seventeenth century. Brucellosis, which causes abortions, must have factored in the disappearance of bison in the late nineteenth century. Today bison are by no stretch of the imagination endangered. There are over 500,000 in the United States. Billionaire and media giant Robert Edward "Ted" Turner owns 45,000 of them, the largest heard in the country, scattered on a number of ranches in many of the western states.[15] Most bison are being raised for commercial purposes, but public herds are everywhere and abundantly enjoyed by visitors from all over the United States and the world.

Grizzly Bears

The story with grizzly bears is very similar to that of wolves, except that bears were never absent; their numbers just became low in both Yellowstone and Glacier National Parks. As in the case of wolves, they were never endangered, just not represented everywhere they used to be. Depending on your source of information, grizzly bears in North America number somewhere between 35,000 and 55,000.[16]

For decades, the bears in Yellowstone and Glacier were allowed to feed in the garbage dumps. This made it easy for tourists to view them and the food source allowed for a lot of bears. However, it was dangerous to have the bears concentrated where the tourists were. In 1967, two young women were killed in separate incidents on the same day. After that, the parks started trucking the garbage away.

Consequently, bear numbers dwindled. In 1993, there were an estimated 136 grizzlies in Yellowstone, and the management goal was set to increase that number to 500. There are currently over 1,000.[17] Note that one reason there are only 108 wolves in Yellowstone is that there are 1,000 bears.

In Glacier and the adjoining wilderness area, there were around 300 in 1997 and the management goal was set to increase that number to 391. Recent surveys counted 765 bears, and these bears are now ranging far from their designated home.[18] In 2017, a pair of young males were captured and euthanized 150 miles east of the mountains. These bears were not only not where they were not supposed to be, but they were killing livestock. Grizzlies now regularly follow the drainages to the east of the Rocky Mountain Front, preying on livestock and endangering residents.

Dangerous encounters between bears and hunters, fishermen, hikers, and ranchers have increased significantly in just the last few years. In 2013, there were 4 encounters with no injuries in the southern area of Montana centered around Yellowstone. By 2019, there were 19 encounters with 5 injuries. For the first part of 2020, the encounter and injury incidents increased again, with 5 people mauled just by June.

As for predation by grizzlies, that, too, is on the increase. The 2019 statistics for the state of Montana show 61 cattle and 52 sheep.[19] In the probable category are another 35 cattle, 13 sheep, 2 guard dogs, 1 horse, and 4 llamas. Again, as in the case of wolves, it is impossible to know the actual numbers lost to bears. Losses are so great that ranchers with grazing permits in the mountains of western Montana are questioning if it is advisable to use those pastures. This will have the further consequence that grass and brush will increase in the mountains, adding to the fuel load for wildfires. Chances are that a number of bears will be killed by forest fires.

The populations agreed upon for the recovery of the grizzly bear have been met and exceeded, but in 2019, when the US Fish and Wildlife Service moved to delist them from the endangered species list, a number of environmental groups sued. Their claim is that there are still not enough bears from a genetic breeding population perspective. In their estimation, bear numbers should be allowed to increase so that bears in Yellowstone and bears in Glacier can freely interbreed.

In order for bears from Yellowstone and Glacier to interbreed, there would be bears anywhere and everywhere in Montana in ever-increasing numbers. In essence, the groups suing to prevent the delisting of grizzlies are promising a bear in everyone's backyard. Since grizzlies are already being sighted nearly everywhere, if you work or recreate where bears might be, it is advisable to go armed. Children running around on the creeks and coulees are at risk. Those suing to block the management of grizzly bears seemingly value the bears more than people.

Magical Thinking and Reality

It would be most magical to see a line of woolly mammoths coming down from the hills across from where my house now stands to water in the creek. Perhaps there would be a saber-toothed tiger lurking to catch some unwary prey. Not that long ago, certainly in the time of the first Native Americans, that would have been a common occurrence, and as I said, it would be a magical thing to witness. Yet, although we can no longer see woolly mammoth or even saber-toothed tigers, we are doing just fine. The world, its people, and nature are going on just fine without them.

Here in Montana, we were doing just fine without wolves before 1995, when they were introduced into Yellowstone. Seeing wolves and grizzly bears in Yellowstone is a thrill, an aesthetic experience, probably not quite as good as it would be to see an actual live woolly mammoth, but still thrilling. Aesthetic experiences, however, are cheap when other people pay the band. Isn't that a definition of selfishness!

The deluge of propaganda that demanded the introduction of apex predators spoke glowingly of the need for increased predation to balance the Yellowstone ecosystem. To some degree, they have done that. As a result of predation, the park's elk population has decreased. Park rangers now regale visitors about the regrowth of brush along the Lamar River and the reappearance of beavers, all because the elk no longer strip the riverbanks free of willows. If it was just about restoring willows and beavers, the elk could have been culled through hunting instead, and ranchers could have been spared wolves killing livestock.

But has the cost for getting willows and beavers into Yellowstone been tabulated by those who continue to advocate in favor of wolves and bears? Increased numbers of predators and their inevitable predation on livestock have alienated the entire rural population of Idaho, Montana, and Wyoming. It may not be the whole story, but I believe the reintroduction of wolves has contributed to the election of ten Republican US senators and representatives from Idaho, Montana, and Wyoming, who deny global warming, oppose a rational renewable energy policy, undermine clean air and water regulations, refuse to hold corporations responsible for pollution, favor the export of coal to China, and advocate for a pipeline to move Canadian shale oil to Texas—all issues important to most conservationists and rational thinkers.

Montana's politics took a decided turn to the right in this past election. Roughly speaking, in the past few decades, the Democrats primarily controlled the state's urban centers and gained the votes of people moving to Montana from the West Coast. The Republicans' base was largely concentrated in small towns and rural areas. The recent transplants to Montana from the West Coast were content to go along with the wolf reintroduction since they presumably saw wolves as a good idea as long as they were off bothering someone else. Having to invest in a bear-proof garbage can and reinforce your garage door is another matter. Worrying whether you should go out in the evening to look at the stars or let your kids run around is even more of a concern. Grizzly bears were an unstated factor in the recent election.

I am writing here as though everyone in rural America is at war with coyotes, wolves, bison, and bears, along with all the rest of nature. That is not so at all. After all, agriculture is an important component of nature, and farmers and ranchers are arguably closer to nature and, by extension, the environment than most everyone else. The inconvenience that wild animals inflict is part of the life and, in a perverse sense, one of the pleasures: mice nesting in your newly restored antique automobile; pack rats chewing up the rawhide trim on your saddle; skunks and raccoons in the dog food; pigeons making a mess in the shop; foxes packing off a chicken; deer in the haystacks. These are all things you put up with as a normal part of life on a farm or ranch.

You even put up with coyotes killing a handful of lambs. However, killing fifty, well, that is a different story. Rural western folk have enough trouble and work. We don't need, or want, more just because some people who don't live here and don't have to deal with the daily inconveniences think it would be a fun adventure to see a wolf or grizzly bear when they take a road trip to the Rocky Mountain West. There is, obviously, a clash of cultures and priorities between the vison of the wildlife partisans and the people who live on the land. Rural people interpret that cultural clash as selfishness and disrespect. It is, you might say, a failure on the part of conservationists/environmentalists to normalize from reality.

The Complicity of Consumers

> Burn down your cities and leave our farms, and your cities will spring up again as if by magic. But destroy our farms and the grass will grow in the streets of every city in the country.
> —William Jennings Bryan, "Cross of Gold" speech, 1896

American consumers have access to the most abundant and inexpensive choices of food ever. Supermarket shelves overflow with fresh and prepared food. Fruits and vegetables that used to be only seasonal are available every day of the year, even if they must be shipped in from halfway around the world—perhaps from the tables of people who may not have enough for themselves.

According to the USDA, in 2018, Americans spent 9.7 percent of their disposable income on food. Forty-eight percent of that was food bought in restaurants.[1] This amount was the least ever, however, because of the COVID-19 pandemic and subsequent inflation that has risen to 11.3 percent in 2022. Fifty years earlier, consumers spent 15.1 percent of their income, and following the end of World War II, the average spent by Americans for food was right at 20 percent.[2]

The cost of raising food has gone up, but farmgate prices, the portion of the food dollar that farmers actually see, has gone down. Farmers have systematically been losing their share of the consumer dollar while processors and retailers have increased their margins. According to statistics published by the National Farmers Union, in 1980, the farmers' share was 37 cents of every dollar spent at retail.[3] By 1997, it was down to 21 cents, and in 2019, the farmers' share was only 14.6 cents.[4] Reforming agricultural markets does not necessarily mean that consumers should or would pay more for food. What the current system of processor cartels and retail giants allows is for these firms to profit by paying less and less for the raw product. The global agro-industrial cartel does not add new value; they simply steal from farmers.

If the main benefit to consumers from industrialized agriculture is cheap food, what is the potential downside? The system that the global cartels administer is predicated on meeting their shareholders' needs, not the needs of society. There is no profit in built-in redundancy. There are no contingencies should a pandemic, an economic meltdown, a war, or climate catastrophes interfere with the supply chains. In fact, all these disasters are, for the cartels, opportunities for higher profits.

Should industrialized agriculture prove to be unable to adapt to global economic turmoil and climatic instability, what other models do we have that could? Many look to organic and regenerative agriculture to be an alternative to agro-industry, but is this realistic? We need some statistics to understand the scale of the issues.

According to the USDA, there are 900 million acres currently being farmed or grazed in the United States; 591.2 million acres of are in grasslands, 66 percent of the total.[5] Another 33 percent of the total, 298.8 million acres, is planted to major commodity crops, such as corn, soybeans, sorghum, wheat, barley, oats, or cotton. This leaves 10.1 million acres, or just 1 percent, that is used for vegetable production. Orchards account for another 1 percent of farmland.

It is those 10.1 million acres that supply vegetables to the supermarkets and farmers' markets. These fields are, for the most part, the best land, with the best rainfall and the best access to irrigation. It is also the most labor-intensive form of agriculture and the type of farming where carbon-rich soils make the greatest difference.

Out of the total land farmed, 308.9 (298.8 + 10.1) million acres, only about 5.5 million acres (1.8 percent) are devoted to organic farming. There are, of course, farms that employ different levels of what are considered sustainable agricultural practices. However, because these farms are hard to define, the USDA does not count them separately, making it hard to fix the actual number of acres in organic and/or sustainable agriculture. But the point is that the overall number of acres devoted to sustainable/regenerative types of farming is very small compared to the totality of agriculture.

It is from this mix of organic and sustainable farming that we get seasonally appropriate fruits and vegetables sold at farmers' markets across the nation. Organic fruits, vegetables, and free-range chickens are perhaps the "best" products coming from agriculture, but they are just a tiny fraction of what is a gigantic industry. Most farmers are tied to the industrial system of food production.

It is not that many farmers would oppose adopting a more eco-friendly form of agriculture, such as that espoused by regenerative farming advocates; rather, it is that there is no easy way to get off the industrialized agrotechnological merry-go-round. Consider this: plant selection and other agrotechnology have more than doubled the yield of an acre of corn in the last fifty years. Today an acre can yield two hundred bushels of corn. That is nearly twelve thousand pounds of corn—six tons an acre. This is a very big pile of corn. For that six tons of corn, a farmer in a good year (a very good year) will gross (not net) $622 dollars.

Believe me, most farmers would love to get off that merry-go-round. But if you are in debt, there is no easy way—you just have to hang on tight and hope for the best. The market price for a bushel of corn (as of 2019) is $3.11, and the cost of raising the corn is $5.41. Four hundred forty-three acres of Iowa land suitable to raise corn costs $3,229,430, plus another $1 million for the machinery. That is a crushing debt load, which has to be paid for by a market system that most years pays less than the cost of production.

It is not any better raising cattle or any other alternative crop. The current price for feeder calves is around $1.50 a pound, and the cost of raising them, $1.75 a pound. A ranch large enough to raise two hundred cows costs up to $5 million and another half a million to stock and equip it. It is fair to ask why anyone would pay that much just to lose money year after year. One reason is that farming and ranching is just as much a cultural identity as it is an economic endeavor. People do not stop identifying with their heritage, even when it is inconvenient. As a result, farmers and ranchers have historically been willing to sacrifice to stay on the land because that is part of who they are, what has been passed down through their families.

One reason that ranchland is so expensive is because multimillionaires bid up prices just so they can have the bragging rights of a place to entertain their hunting buddies. Taxpayers even subsidize multimillionaires by allowing tax deductions for putting a conservation easement on the land. Only those with sizable nonfarm income are able to use that particular tax dodge. It is a certainly not a useful write-off for a young beginning ranch couple whose main concern is to make a living by raising cattle.

Industrial Agribusiness

The captains of industry have no reason to question what they are doing or second-guess the control they hold over production agriculture. After all, they are applying the principles taught to them in the prestigious schools of business administration. They implement the neoliberal agenda as it was taught to them. The internal logic of neoliberalism forces the outcome in the direction of greater and greater centralized control by global corporations.

But the COVID-19 epidemic caused cracks to appear in the food chain, particularly in the way meat is processed. For a period in 2020, not only were the supermarket shelves devoid of toilet paper, but the meat case was also empty. There are only 548 plants in this country that slaughter and process nearly all of the chickens, hogs, and cattle. These plants employ a mostly immigrant, nonunionized, low-paid workforce. The line speeds that govern the frequency at which each carcass comes past each worker allows just seconds to accomplish the assigned task.

Because the workers are literally shoulder to shoulder, the COVID-19 virus swept through these packing plants. According to a June 2021 report by the United Food and Commercial Workers International Union, 58,856 meat-packing workers tested positive for COVID-19, with 297 deaths.[6] If for any reason one of these plants shut down, which did indeed happen, there were immediate repercussions up and down the supply chain. Live animals cannot be just put in storage until the plant is ready to start up again. The system is designed so that when one pen of livestock exits the growing/fattening facility, a new group enters.

It would be one thing if packing plants were small and dispersed, instead of mammoth. Out-of-control COVID-19 infections in one pork-packing facility in Sioux Falls, South Dakota (Smithfield—now owned by a Chinese company), caused it to close for two weeks. This one plant slaughters, processes, and markets 5 percent of all of hogs in the United States. The dictates of efficiency are such that the plants function at capacity, resulting in a limited ability to adjust when even a single plant shuts down. There is literally no place for the animals to go.

Farmers growing hogs had a gut-wrenching situation. The barns were full of 250-pound pigs ready for slaughter with no place to go and nothing to do but eat and get bigger. Meanwhile, the sows were having piglets that could not enter the feeding stage because there was no space. The only solution was to kill those baby pigs and dispose of them in a landfill. No one seems to have kept track of the numbers euthanized, but according to knowledgeable sources, it ran into the millions.[7]

But it was not just animals being sacrificed—it was people too. Packing plant workers were naturally apprehensive about going to work and demanded that they be allowed to draw unemployment benefits, the same as waiters and bartenders who could not work because of restaurant and bar closures. To prevent a walkout of their workers, the meat cartel appealed to President Trump, who made the following statement:

> We're going to sign an executive order today, I believe. And that will solve any liability problems where they have certain liability problems, and we'll be in very good shape. We're working with Tyson, which is one of the big companies in the world. And we always work with the farmers. There's plenty of supply, as you know. There's plenty of

supply. It's distribution. And we will probably have that today solved. It was a very unique circumstance, because of liability.[8]

The president invoked the Defense Production Act, declaring that packing plant workers could not qualify for unemployment benefits because they were essential workers and, furthermore, the companies were shielded from liability for providing an unsafe working environment. According to various news reports, the packing cartel did not even lose money the year that caused so much physical, psychic, and economic pain to millions of Americans, not to mention death. The spread between what beef-packers paid for cattle and what they were able to sell the beef for increased by 323 percent.[9]

During the first half of 2021, the packing cartel bought fat cattle for $1,700 per head and sold the meat two weeks later for $2,700, totaling a $1,000 markup. In a July 2021 Senate hearing, executives from Tyson and JBS, two of the largest companies of the meat cartel, explained that this was just a matter of supply and demand. Their reasoning was that because of slowdowns in the slaughter plants, there was a surplus of cattle on the market, causing lower cattle prices. Meanwhile, this resulted in less beef available to consumers, making for an increase in demand, which in turn meant higher beef prices. Supply and demand is a convenient excuse when you control the bottleneck.

What we witnessed is the logical result of the neoliberal (or, if you like, nouveau fascist) doctrine. Some of the poorest and most vulnerable people in the United States are required by our government to work and risk death. The alternative is that the edifice of cards that is our agricultural industrial system risked crashing down around our ears.

A Historical Perspective

To understand how we came to have a food system dominated by global agro-industry, a little historical context may be helpful. After the leaders of the new Soviet Union consolidated their hold on urban areas and factories during the Russian Revolution, they turned their attention to rural Russia. Under the czars, Russia had a feudal system rife with inequality. The policies Vladimir Lenin and then Joseph Stalin implemented were simple—kill or exile all the independent landowning farmers. The next step was to consolidate the farmworkers into collectives with politically reliable bureaucrats in charge. Unsurprisingly, the result was famine in which millions died. Under the centrally directed, scientifically modern collective farm system, the Soviet Union was never able to fully feed itself, even though Russia has some of the best farmland in Europe.

The course of farming in America took a very different route during the same time period. Coming out of World War I and while Russian farmers were being murdered, rural America went into an economic depression. The 1920s roared in the cities, but in the country, people groaned. Conditions got even worse in the 1930s, when everywhere, the cities included, was depressed. In Montana, as in many parts of the West, farms were simply abandoned, and the land reverted to the government.

It took World War II to put farmers back on their feet. Agriculture was designated an essential industry for the war effort, and farmers were exempted from the draft. Most young men enlisted anyway, and running the farm was left to the older men and the women. Guaranteed prices boosted yields, and the American food production system and associated rural communities came out of World War II in the best shape ever.

Following the war, agrotechnology also came into its own. The land-grant university research stations went to work selecting plant and animal varieties for greater productivity. Herbicides, pesticides, and fertilizers came onto the market. Farm machinery was greatly improved. In 1950, there were just over five million farms, averaging 216 acres in size. Twelve percent of the US population lived and worked on these farms.

The average farm of 1950 was just what one would expect. Old MacDonald's farm was diversified. The main crop was determined by where the farm was located: cotton in Mississippi, wheat in the Great Plains, and corn in Iowa. But almost every farm had a few beef cows and a milk cow, some pigs, a flock of chickens, and a large garden. The main cash crop paid, or didn't pay as the case might be, the mortgage. The family, however, lived off the side crops—eggs, cream, tomatoes, etc.—sold to pay for basic needs. The market for these homegrown products was local, while the main crop went into a regional market.

But the agrotechnology resulted in surpluses, particularly corn. Market prices crashed. The government responded with subsidies, but that only resulted in more surpluses. The government then required acreage set-asides in order for farmers to qualify for the subsidy. But farmers aren't stupid—they set aside their least fertile land, and advances in agrotechnology continued to result in ever greater harvests. The government then responded with an insane solution: they concluded, like the commissars in the Soviet Union had previously decided, that the problem was the farmers themselves.

If the smaller farms could be induced to go out of business, so-called dynamic farmers would consolidate the land into "efficient units." Since these "efficient" farmers, as the USDA and the agricultural economists reasoned, would have "economies of scale," the problem of ever more expensive subsidies would disappear. Successive secretaries of agriculture made no bones about it: "We must eliminate more of the human resources from agriculture," is what Earl Butz, the secretary of agriculture under the Nixon administration, openly said.

This policy was "effective" in one respect—they succeeded in eliminating much of the human resources from agriculture. However, the profitability part never materialized, and the cost to the government never went down. In recent years, all they have managed to do is hide the subsidies under another name—crop insurance. But without this nonsubsidy subsidy, the modern "efficient" farmer cannot stumble from one planting season to the next.

The other effect of the "eliminate the farmer policy" was to hollow out rural America: no farmers, no businesses, no jobs, no children, no schools—no communities. As of 2019, the USDA reported that there are just over 2 million farms with an average size of 443 acres. But this figure hides a different reality: 209,007 farms produce 78.7 percent of the total sales. A full half of what are called farms are homes sitting on enough acres to qualify for lower agricultural property taxes. That leaves 785,300 actual family farms. Overall, less than 1 percent of the US population is actively engaged in farming.

Among the 209,007 largest farms are ones that do not resemble a farm in any manner. They are, instead, animal-production factories. And this American system is directed not by a central committee of political commissars but by the board of directors of a rather small number of firms that dominate the manufacture and distribution of inputs and the purchasing and processing of the resulting harvests. "Too big to fail" banks and hedge funds provide the capital, and government enforces the rules.

This corporate agricultural system is predicated on uniformity and monoculture. Without a dependable supply of cheap corn and soybeans, the factories of chickens, pigs, and cows would falter, as would many other aspects of the food and energy system. This nation's food system, particularly chicken, pork, and beef, and including ethanol, is all predicated on corn and soybeans being available for less than the cost of production. The system is brittle, as would be any system in which the underlying economics are fraudulent and the control and decision-making are excessively concentrated.

There are worrisome indicators that all might not be rosy for the future of industrialized agriculture. The big one, of course, is the weather. With climate change, weather patterns have gotten highly unpredictable. Farming and livestock production depend on a certain level of climatic consistency. It is easy to speculate that, if the world gets warmer, the corn belt would shift to the north. Wheat would shift even farther north, and cotton and sorghum would shift to where corn used to be. But that is if the weather changes in a consistent and predictable manner. But if one year is hot as blazes such that the corn crop can't pollinate properly, and the next year is cold and wet and the tractors can't get into the fields until it is too late, we have a problem.

Other problematic things are also happening. One of the firms that controls the supply of critical inputs is Monsanto (now owned by Bayer), who developed the herbicide Roundup (glyphosate) and the GMO seed technology that makes its proprietary seeds immune to the effects of Roundup. Corn, soybeans, and weeds are becoming resistant to Roundup. In the case of corn and soybeans, that initially was the point, but now farmers are getting feral corn in their soybean fields and feral soybeans in their cornfields, and weeds in both.

The thing about Roundup is that it is the essential ingredient in no-till agriculture. Tilling—plowing—was, of course, one of the big breakthroughs that made agriculture possible in the first place. That is how farmers minimize weeds in their crop. But plowing makes the soil vulnerable to wind and water erosion. It also accelerates the process of oxidation of soil carbon, the little bits of plant material that makes soil fertile. No-till farming, using Roundup to eliminate weeds, is common in just about every major crop, even those not using genetically modified seeds.

Roundup was/is the magic ingredient, even if it is losing its effectiveness as weeds increasingly become resistant to its lethal effects. More worrisome, it is now looking likely that Monsanto hid the fact from the world that glyphosate is also poisonous to humans. That little tidbit is currently working its way through the legal system. Scientists are finally getting access to the raw data, because the courts are allowing plaintiffs access to information previously considered proprietary and, therefore, hidden from independent verification.[10] If glyphosate is pulled from the market, the effects on agriculture would be severe.

The third issue that is increasing the vulnerability of modern agriculture is a side effect of globalization. With the increasing international flow of people and food products comes disease. Chicken and hog factories must now maintain sterile procedures, just like a hospital isolation unit. Avian flu, swine flu, and African swine fever are just a few of the infections that could eliminate millions of chickens and pigs overnight. Plants, too, have their pathogens and insects that are spreading around the world.

So between the uncertain and increasingly frightening changes in climate, the unraveling of the agrotechnology that has made monoculture and factory farms workable, and the increasing threat of introduced diseases, what we have come to take for granted in our food production system could come tumbling down.

Myths and Half Truths

These are worrisome trends about the future of food security under the agro-industrial system, but are there alternative models available to pick up the slack should industrialized agriculture falter? This, too, is problematic. A body of half notions has penetrated the public consciousness. These half notions are not meant to be malicious, but agriculture is complicated. What works, or may even work brilliantly, in one microclimate may not be the least bit appropriate, or effective, in another. In short, no panacea exists.

One idea that is currently making its way among concerned consumers and organic/natural farmers is soil carbon sequestration, sometimes called "regenerative" farming. The central idea is that soils around the world have become depleted of soil carbon, reducing soils' fertility and ability to hold rainwater. Many believe that if agricultural methods were more sensitive to this problem, soils could hold a lot more carbon, perhaps enough to even stop global warming. This is obviously an exciting possibility if it is realistic.

The big enemy of soil carbon is the sun. In tropical areas, the soil, even in the middle of a rain forest, has nearly no soil carbon, because warmth accelerates the action of microorganisms and insects in digesting cellulose. At the other end of the world, a lot of carbon becomes incorporated into the soil in the arctic tundra. Peat bogs such as those in Ireland and Scotland are ancient, accumulated soil carbon. It stays there, sequestered for as long as the peat is not disturbed. If the world is getting warmer, which seems to be the case, that obviously works against the sequestration of carbon in soils.

One way to promote carbon sequestration in farm ground is to not plow very often. No-till farming is what is needed. There are not many ways to practice no-till farming. We have already talked about chemical no-till. Another, natural way is to convert farmland to hay and livestock pasture—in other words, raise more cattle and sheep. Right there we have a cognitive dissonance, since another faction of concerned conservationists fervently believes that sheep and cattle significantly harm the environment. But this notion is also the result of misinformation.

In Montana, large acreages of farmland were converted to livestock production about fifty years ago, before anyone was particularly concerned about carbon sequestration. The homestead era that started in this part of Montana during the early twentieth century resulted in a lot of native grassland plowed under to raise wheat, barley, and oats. That era and its associated farming practices collapsed in the Dust Bowl and Depression of the 1930s. The surviving farmers consolidated the best land and continued farming, in part because US farm policy gave them subsidies to plant. But when government policy changed, requiring a certain percentage of each farm to be kept fallow, the less productive fields were converted to hay or pasture.

There are still a lot of field crops raised in Montana on the better soils and where irrigation allows for intensive farming. Most of these crops are raised under no-till production using Roundup. The rest, the least fertile, is now converted to improved pasture planted with a mixture of alfalfa and grass. There is not much one can do to improve the sequestration of soil carbon in these fields, as this is already the formula.

Raising field crops in Montana has always been problematic. The limiting ingredient is rainfall. This is why summer fallow became the norm. Through summer fallow, two years' worth of rainfall can be concentrated in one crop. A fall/winter cover crop, which is the prescription for building soil carbon and controlling weeds in the regenerative farming model, requires moisture that in much of the arid plains is simply not available.

There are, however, areas of this nation, other than Montana, where annual rainfall is enough to allow for year-round cropping. It is in these places where carefully targeted farming practices, such as winter cover crops, can minimize the proliferation of weeds without resorting to herbicides or plowing. But it is not easy, and it does not come without associated trade-offs and costs. Certainly, soil-friendly regenerative farming is worth doing where feasible, but expecting soil-friendly farming to seamlessly replace Roundup-dependent industrialized farming, and still maintain the high yields and low prices is not realistic.

More about Regenerative Agriculture

What regenerative farming partisans also envision is a complete transformation of how agriculture is currently structured. Instead of agriculture reliant on expensive chemicals and fertilizers, soil-friendly farming practices would naturally increase the fertility and water-absorbing capacity of America's agricultural landscapes. This would result in more carbon removed from the atmosphere and a transformation of agriculture to a diversified farming system—a reversion to the past where rural communities were more vibrant because agriculture was conducted by family farmers, not corporate executives.

However, proponents of regenerative farming have so far provided no clear path on how to make this paradigm shift. The regenerative farming techniques that are proposed are essentially practices developed in gardening and truck farming, scaled up to field agriculture. It is true that given a farm located where there is adequate rainfall, these techniques can be effective. But in other environments, especially drier ones, many of the promoted practices are not particularly appropriate.

Then, too, nothing is proven as to costs and yields of regenerative agriculture. To my knowledge, there are no side-by-side comparative field tests. The testimonials I have seen, or heard, are largely anecdotal. I am not saying that there are no farmers who successfully practice the techniques of regenerative agriculture, but they are, by necessity, financially independent. If you are a beginning farmer applying for a bank loan, the loan officer will want to see a healthy projected cash flow and strongly suggest that you follow the norms of the industrial agricultural system, because industrial farming has a proven, reproducible track record.

It is not clear that nonagricultural people, including policymakers (i.e., the congressional representatives advocating the Green New Deal), understand the complexities. The regenerative advocates tend to focus on technical farming practices rather than necessary policy reforms. This makes it likely that the message heard by non-farming people is that the economic problems faced by agriculture are technical in nature and not structural, such as those caused by market dysfunction. I can just hear some environmentally minded person muttering that if farmers were not so pigheaded, they would adopt regenerative methodologies and all rural economic issues would sort themselves out.

As mentioned above, the regenerative agriculture enthusiast provides a vision but not a road map. The trail between here and there is rough, with numerous collapsed bridges. Global industrial agriculture is premised on marketing proprietary chemicals to large farms and purchasing the resulting food through noncompetitive, corporate-owned marketplaces. Until that fact is addressed, reform in American agriculture through regenerative techniques, or anything else, is questionable.

Short-Duration, High-Intensity Range Management

Another concept, closely related to regenerative agriculture, that has become "mainstream," so to speak, is Holistic Resource Management (HRM), a set of techniques to manage livestock by "regenerating grasslands from an ecological, economic, and social perspective."[11] Zimbabwean research biologist and game ranger Allan Savory developed HRM, arguing that grazing animals and grasslands have coevolved. Grass depends on grazing animals just as much as the animals depend on grass. Another of his insights, although certainly not his alone, is that it is better for the health of the grass if it is grazed only once, late in its growing phase. His model is based on how large groups of wildlife move across the plains of Africa, consume what is before them in a day or two, and then move on.

One corollary that particularly caught the attention of livestock producers is that if you manage this holistic grazing system properly, you can potentially raise more animals than is feasible under a system in which the livestock are allowed to graze indiscriminately over an entire season. In fact, Savory insists that greater grazing density is an absolute requirement.[12] Personally, I have observed that this is true in certain microclimates, not particularly true in others, and not true at all in some. What works on the southern plains of Texas—where there is a long growing season and rains that periodically stimulate the regrowth of grass—has limited application on the eastern plains of Montana, where there is only one short period of growth for native grasses. Then consider even more arid places where the rains are so episodic that you really don't know when grass will be available to livestock, and once that is gone, it is gone, not to reappear until it rains again.

The big practical problem, say, in the last example of an arid microclimate, is where to keep livestock in the periods between the rains. The sheep and cows have to graze somewhere, possibly overgrazing those pastures. The HRM system can be dogmatic and not at all easy to implement. In Montana, many ranchers have looked at HRM, and a good number have made it work, but even more ranchers have concluded that it is not practical in their circumstances.

For instance, the notion that one should increase the number of grazing animals during times of good rains and decrease them when there is a threat of drought is problematic. First, you have to have money in your bank account in order to buy cows in the good years. If you are relying on the good will of a banker to lend you money, that is a problem, as they tend not to like what looks to them as speculation. Then, too, it takes many years of breeding and selection to get the right cows for your operation. If you sell them on the bad year and expect to buy back the same quality on the good, well, you can forget about it. Finally, if you are leasing land, especially from the government, the lessor will never authorize more cows than what has been calculated as the standard stocking rate.

Many Montana ranchers have looked at the HRM system and concluded that it just was not practical for them. The standard wisdom of range management in Montana—use half and leave half—works pretty well. HRM might be better but not enough to warrant the time or investment. But nonranchers, having heard about the wonders of HRM, might conclude that ranchers not on the HRM bandwagon are hopelessly ignorant and uneducated. However, what these people should consider is that if something that seems obvious is not happening, then perhaps there is a good reason.

The Future of Food Production

Industrialized monoculture will probably not simply collapse overnight. Multinational corporate control of agricultural markets is nearly total and they have the money and power to use government and your taxes to prop up agriculture when things turn sour—at least as long as the corporations are still making money. This is probably for the good, considering we are not very well prepared with a working alternative model. Organic and/or regenerative agriculture has been growing over the last half a century, but it would take magical thinking to believe that it can be a realistic substitute for industrial agriculture.

But industrialized agriculture is still vulnerable, and it may not require a complete collapse to throw our nation's food security into turmoil. Successive bad corn harvests, resulting from unpredictable weather, could send everything into a tailspin. Higher corn prices might be good for the corn farmers, at least those with a crop to sell, but there are downstream economic consequences to livestock feeders, ethanol factories, users of corn oil, the fructose industry, and the buyers of the more esoteric corn-derived additives that are the key ingredients in many, many processed food products. Higher corn prices would have broad economic repercussions.

Industrialized agriculture is the way it is because monopolistic corporations control inputs and outputs and only allow the illusion of market competition. This is what global capitalism has created for us in a number of industries—the illusion of market competition. Walmart is cheaper than Sears, but Amazon is cheaper than both. At the retail level, we may have market competition, but cheaper is not always better, and it is almost impossible in today's retail market to distinguish quality from junk.

Banking, airlines, petroleum, the internet, mobile phone service, health insurance, and pharmaceuticals, just to name a few, are all industries in which competition is compromised. And behind that, at the level of global finance and decision-making and at the level of who pays taxes and who does not, competition is all smoke and mirrors. The exceedingly rich get richer while the rest of the world gets poorer. But it does not have to play out that way. Our economic and social problems are because of the policy choices we—as a nation—have collectively made.

Conclusion: What Should We Do?

It is normal for people to want their cake and eat it too, along with the icing and all of the little candy decorations. People want good food, but naturally they want to pay as little as possible. So, does it matter if the cost for food is less than the cost to raise it, and if so, what are the implications?

American consumers pay the least amount, as a percentage of disposable income, for their food as ever in our history, and a lot of that food comes preprepared in delis or restaurants. Farmers receive less for their work than ever (37 cents of every food dollar in 1980 versus 14.6 cents today). So why shouldn't American consumers want their cake and eat it too? No one has ever told them that this was not possible or that it was not their right. But there may come a time when the realities become irreconcilable.

We now have an agricultural system controlled by a global agro-industry, which oversees a farming system dependent on exploitation of everything it touches: the farmers, the farmworkers, the animals, the water, the soil, and the food itself. They have accomplished this by subverting the free exchange of information that is supposed to come through a transparent, competitive market system. The trade-off is that food is cheap—at least for the time being.

Yet even in a land of plenty, people are hungry, prompting many to be concerned about how much food Americans waste. But why would consumers not waste food if it is so cheap as to be nearly valueless? Consider this—a fifty-pound sack of corn is cheaper than fifty pounds of wood pellets to burn in a wood-burning furnace. One is food, and the other is sawdust. Doesn't that suggest something is off kilter?

People also want recreational experiences that are as magnificent as possible, and if it comes free, all the better. The issue of wildlife and places where wildlife can conduct their lives as Mother Nature first dictated, is, in this twenty-first century, rife with conflicting interests and emotions. None of us, not even hard-bitten old ranchers, are immune to the spell of watching a coyote or a mountain lion, or even the common everyday progressions of deer. The fascination most certainly is built in. It is part of our DNA.

But where should that wildlife be allowed to do their thing? To my knowledge, no one proposed to reintroduce wolves to New York's Central Park, where they could subsist on rats, pigeons, and off-leash dogs. No, instead the wolf advocates thought that Yellowstone would be the perfect place. It is large and surrounded by even more national forest. If the wolves were to venture beyond these borders, well, that is nature and the workings of biodiversity at its best. Besides, I expect that many feel that since farmers and ranchers already host a number of wild animals, what is one more in their role as stewards of the land? You might say that the presumption is that farmers and ranchers have a civic duty to participate in biodiversity for the benefit of all.

That is the problem—the underlying selfishness. One of my questions in this essay is, "Where are the natural limits to this selfishness?" I do not see the current system of industrialized farming as sustainable. I say this while acknowledging that America's farmers, under the yoke of multinational agribusiness, are producing food at a volume and price never experienced. I also do not believe that the regenerative and sustainable methodologies of farming are capable of the same level of productivity.

But, undeniably, the system is being stressed. Will it break? I think the chances are that it will—crisis is inevitable. The only alternative I can see to mitigate the ill effects is to devolve our farming system to one that resembles that of the 1950s—more farmers on smaller farms with more flexibility in crops raised, and most important of all, markets that are local and truly competitive. Without a competitive market system to price farm commodities, farmers and consumers of food will not be able to communicate efficiently on the real needs of society.

In the process of reorienting our food-production industry, it is not a matter of feeling sorry for the poor, put-upon farmer. They—we—have made our choices just like everyone else. Sure, farmers work hard, but so does everybody else. The person to be most concerned about is ultimately yourself, because a crisis in food production will affect you.

Ideally, just as with curbing the production of greenhouse gases, we should begin early to ensure the future of food security. It would be better to have a planned evolution than a climate-forced collapse of industrialized agriculture. But we will not get anywhere at all if America's urban population and America's farmers continue a protracted cultural war over issues that are frankly peripheral to the looming national food crisis.

My son, Antoine, on horseback, when he was about four years old. My wife Joan passed away in 2003. We were married for twenty-nine years.

(*above*) This picture of a bull elephant with a spear piercing his trunk was taken in Kenya's Amboseli National Park in 2008.

(*below*) Ewe with triplets.

In the fall of 1964, I was a freshman at Rocky Mountain College in Billings, Montana.

(right) I must have been about six in this picture with ducklings.

(below) In April 2022, I testified at the US Capitol before the House Committee on Agriculture.

In 1999, in conjunction with protests in Seattle against the undemocratic proceeding of the World Trade Organization, a number of organizations led by the Northern Plains Resource Council organized a symbolic blockade of the border crossing from Canada into Montana, because Canada was dumping cattle into the US market. I was one of the speakers.

Here I am overlooking my ranch from the ridge to the north of the buildings.

This was taken at Lake Nakuru in Kenya in 2007. Nona was visiting me while I was working for the US Agency for International Development in East Africa. Nona and I got married in 2010.

Grandma and her brood. My grandfather died in 1920, just before the birth of my father. Grandma was on her own raising her four little children.

Nona's two sons, John and Matt, along with Matt's soon-to-be wife, Tess, crossing the creek on the ranch. Unfortunately, John's wife, Paloma, is not in this picture.

Here I am in about 1990 looking over MacDonald Creek Valley.

(*above*) One summer Nona and I raised a magpie, whom we called Maggie. It was a fun encounter, and here we are pressing apples together. In the fall, Maggie joined the wild magpies. I hope she is doing well.

(*below*) Getting this little buckskin colt accustomed to me.

(above) My brother, Charles, and I with our mother, about 1956.

(below) My parents, Bill and Elvia, and I in Paris. In 1948, my father attended art school in Paris. My mother and I had the opportunity to spend that year with our French family.

In 1877, the Nez Percé attempted to avoid capture by the US Army by escaping to Canada. In this heroic endeavor, they passed through central Montana. This is my father's depiction of that exodus. His preferred artistic style was more abstract, so this is an outlier in his body of work.

Nona and I riding the ridge to check on cattle.

(*above*) A happy flock of sheep on their bed-ground in the morning.

(*below*) These ewes have just spent the night sheltering from a blizzard. Their heavy coats of wool kept them reasonably comfortable.

(*opposite above*) Here I am sorting calves to be branded and vaccinated.

(*opposite below*) Two cows with their twins. It is relatively rare, and not necessarily a good thing, for cows to have twins. Generally, range cattle do not produce enough milk for two and at the same time maintain their own nutritional needs.

(*above*) My grandparents William and Julia met in 1913. He was surveying the new railroad spur in MacDonald Creek Valley and she was looking for a homestead.

In 2008, Willie Nelson held a concert in Missoula, Montana, where we held a joint press conference advocating for saving the family farm system.

The Not COOL Story of the Farm Policy Debate

Most agriculture producers are conservative by nature, and many were enthusiastic that the Trump presidency would deliver needed reform to rural America. His tough talk about trade with China, but also with Canada and Mexico, raised hopes that imports of beef would be curbed, since beef imports are killing the US cattle market. But nothing changed despite all the bluster. Now it is the Democrats and President Joseph Biden's turn. So far, expectations have been exceeded, as a number of needed actions have been proposed. But will proposals and good intentions result in actual reforms?

The right wing is having fun ridiculing the Green New Deal, a plan advanced by Representative Alexandria Ocasio-Cortez (D-NY). Clearly, the strategy is to belittle everything a Democrat proposes as socialism, while contributing very little useful to the dialogue. As for the Green New Deal, it appears to be a wish list of good intentions but not a lot of real legislative meat. It ends with the following promise:

> Providing all people of the United States with—(i) high-quality health care; (ii) affordable, safe, and adequate housing; (iii) economic security; and (iv) clean water, clean air, healthy and affordable food, and access to nature.[1]

While this clause may be a nice reminder of what is important and currently not available to many Americans, when it comes to specifics, the Green New Deal is disappointing. In the agriculture section, it calls for working collaboratively with farmers to remove pollution and greenhouse gas emissions, investing in sustainable farming practices, and promoting land use practices that increase soil health. In short, the Green New Deal does not provide us with practical solutions to guide us to a more resilient food production system.

Much better is what Senators Cory Booker (D-NJ), Elizabeth Warren (D-MA), and Bernie Sanders (I-VT) have proposed in legislation that has the rather cumbersome summary "A Bill to Place a Moratorium on Large Concentrated Animal Feeding Operations, to Strengthen the Packers and Stockyards Act, 1921, to Require Country of Origin Labeling on Beef, Pork and Dairy Products, and for Other Purposes." Mercifully, the short title is the Farm System Reform Act of 2021. Most of its proposed provisions are solid, promising to reform industry practices that livestock producers have been demanding for decades.

Moratorium on Large CAFOs

I am doubtful, however, that the call by Senator Booker et al. for a moratorium on the construction of new large Concentrated Animal Feeding Operations (CAFOs) is legal. In many respects, this would seem to be a good idea, as it is logical that the larger a CAFO, the greater the impact on the landscape and the greater the potential for pollution, should the manure containment system fail in a violent storm. However, how can the federal government, on the basis of size alone, require that a company desist in their business plans if they are otherwise complying with local, state, and federal regulations?

The federal government has jurisdiction over navigable waters, and pollution of rivers by CAFOs are a constant concern. The Obama administration tried to expand that authority over all flowing water through the Waters of the United States (WOTUS) proposal. The Trump administration reversed that regulatory effort and, in so doing, got cheers in rural America because most people in agriculture agree that WOTUS was regulatory overreach. The problem lies that in trying to regulate large corporations, the federal government would have been overregulating the miniscule.

Farmers and ranchers are constantly doing things that may have violated WOTUS yet have no impact on overall water quality. It is in the nature of what we do in raising food—machinery crossing coulees and streams makes temporary messes. Besides, there are already countless county, state, and federal regulations controlling what can or cannot be done that affects the flow of streams. Another set of bureaucrats to check in with was not perceived to be a good idea. We are yet to see what the Biden administration will do about WOTUS.

As with WOTUS, using federal power to control large-scale agriculture impacts the small farms as well, even when those sources of disturbances to the environment are completely transitory. Regulations that impose standards designed to mitigate impacts are important, but that is largely a local and state responsibility. It also seems misplaced to bolster federal regulations without first mending inspection systems. Too much of our inspection capability on food, health, environment, and worker safety has been compromised. The agencies charged with regulating industry are chronically underfunded, and many appear to have been captured by those very same industries they are supposed to regulate. Reform and proper funding of regulatory agencies would be a good place for the federal government and Senator Booker to start.

Besides, what would a moratorium on the construction of large CAFOs accomplish? The reason that more and more poultry, hog, and cattle feeding happens in very large CAFOs is because this is how the economics of animal agriculture is currently structured. A handful of corporations dominate and control the markets. Until that is addressed, the economic pressure will remain for more large feedlots, dairy operations, hog-fattening complexes, and poultry factories.

Captive Supply Reform

While I question the proposed CAFO regulations, other provisions in Senator Booker's Farm Systems Reform Act would address the monopolization of the livestock industry and do so on much more solid legal ground. The Packers and Stockyards Act of 1921 (P&S Act) is the strongest of the antitrust laws, and regulates, or is supposed to regulate, the market activities of poultry-, hog-, and beef-packers.

The P&S Act grew out of the impact of *The Jungle* by Upton Sinclair. In this novel, the author reveals the horrendous living conditions of the packing plant workforce in the hopes of sparking reform. Instead, the readers of that era focused on the unsanitary slaughter and food preparation conditions described in the book. The five-firm cartel (Armour, Swift, Wilson, Morris, and Cudahy) slaughtered 70 percent of the beef and hogs in America, so most consumers were eating meat that came from filthy packing facilities. Because of the public outcry, the Federal Meat Inspection Act, the Food and Drug Administration (FDA), and the Packers and Stockyards Administration were created.

The market practice when *The Jungle* was published was for packing company livestock buyers to inform cattle and hog producers what they were willing to pay for the live animals. As a result of the P&S Act, the packer cartel was required to bid in a public auction. The P&S Act did not break up the packer cartel, but because of increased market competition, as of 1972, the four largest firms, which still included Armour and Swift, controlled just 26 percent of the market.

During the Reagan administration, enforcement of the P&S Act was essentially stopped. As a result, within two decades, four firms gained control of 85 percent of the cattle market, with Armour and Swift turned into subsidiaries of much larger conglomerates. Senator Booker's bill reintroduces a proposal first advanced by the Western Organization of Resource Councils that would require packers once again bid in a public competitive forum for their livestock needs. This worked in 1921, and it should work just as effectively one hundred years later.

The GIPSA Rules

Senator Booker's Farm System Reform Act also calls for the restoration of a set of regulatory interpretations of the P&S Act that would prevent discriminatory and unfair practices experienced by the poultry and hog contract growers. Under the Obama administration, the USDA issued regulatory interpretations of the Grain

Inspection Packers and Stockyards Administration (GIPSA) rules that enumerated the practices that poultry and hog integrators could no longer impose on the contract growers. For instance, it gave the growers the right to witness the weighing of the livestock, protection from arbitrary changes in contract terms, and the right to sue in a court of law.[2]

The GIPSA rules had one more clarification that went to the heart of what constitutes fair market competition. For some reason, the federal courts interpret the P&S Act to say that for a livestock producer to successfully sue a packer for unfair or discriminatory actions, the grower must prove harm to overall competition, not just harm to themselves. This is an absurd standard, as it effectively nullifies the use of the P&S Act as protection for producers from unjustified and discriminatory actions by the dominant packers.

The P&S Act, as interpreted by the Obama administration, clarified that producers do not have to prove competitive harm to the entire industry, but the Trump administration rescinded these GIPSA rules. Senator Booker's bill calls for a restoration of the rules.

Country of Origin Labeling and Reform of "Product of USA" Label

Booker's bill also calls for the restoration of mandatory Country of Origin Labeling (COOL) for beef and pork. The requirement to label beef and pork at retail was voided by Congress in 2015, even though lamb, seafood, poultry, fresh produce, and everything else—even our underwear!—carry a country of origin label.[3] The excuse given was that a World Trade Organization (WTO) tribunal ruled that COOL was discriminatory toward beef and pork produced in Canada or Mexico. Immediately following the elimination of COOL, the prices for cattle collapsed, not because more meat was imported from Canada and Mexico but because more meat was imported from Nicaragua, Brazil, and Australia.[4] The producers in Canada and Mexico, who had insisted their governments file the trade action, effectively shot themselves in the foot because the resulting low cattle prices affect them too.

The elimination of COOL allows for imported beef to sell on a par with US beef because consumers mistake the USDA inspection label to mean that the beef is of US origin. For instance, much of the beef currently sold as "grass fed" comes from Australia or Nicaragua, where the beef importers can purchase the beef for less and sell it at a premium to American consumers, who believe the cattle were born and raised in the United States. Ranchers in this country who would like to sell grass-fed beef cannot get retail shelf space because this is not in the interests of the packing cartel, which also owns the packing plants in Nicaragua, Brazil, and Australia. As a result of the elimination of COOL, tens of billions of dollars is extracted from US ranchers and cattle feeders by the dominant beef-packers.[5]

To make matters worse, consumers are led to believe they are purchasing American-grown beef or pork because USDA allows a "Product of USA" label to be placed on imported meat as long as it has been *repackaged* in this country. This practice is just plain consumer fraud, and the Booker bill calls for that particular "loophole" to be closed.

The principles at stake are quite clear. Consumers have the right to know the origin of their beef and pork purchases. Livestock producers have the right to a fair and transparent market. Reinstating COOL and eliminating the "Product of USA" label are important steps toward restoring free and fair markets, a move that would benefit both producers and consumers.

Other Initiatives

The calls for the restoration of fair and transparent markets in the beef and pork segments of American agriculture have seriously heated up, prompting a number of proposals from members of both political parties and President Biden. Many of the senators and representatives from rural states recognize that something has to be done. The question is what?

Things are moving fast, or at least as fast as is possible in Washington, DC. President Biden has issued an executive order instructing the USDA to fix the "Product of USA" loophole.[6] Senators Jon Tester (D-MT), Mike Rounds (R-SD), and John Thune (R-SD) have joined with Senator Booker in calling for a restoration of COOL.

Another area being scrutinized is the reporting of prices paid for livestock.[7] When farmers and ranchers do not have clear knowledge of current market sales, they are at a disadvantage negotiating with the buyers from the packer cartel. However, the current mandatory price reporting law is limited in what packers are required to report, leaving the overall price discovery process crippled from lack of timely information. The USDA publishes negotiated spot market prices but not the prices for 70–80 percent of cattle sold. A spot market is one where the cattle are sold for cash and delivery is immediate. Each transaction in a spot market is negotiated in a nonpublic forum. By law, the result of these negotiations must be reported to the USDA; however, because the packers successfully argued that since there are only four of them, the prices each individual packer offers is part of a confidential marketing strategy. In other words, the packer cartel contends that because they are an oligopsony, they deserve special treatment in protecting their marketing strategies from the people with whom they are negotiating for livestock. One of the proposals coming from Congress is to expand mandatory market reporting to all purchases. It is unclear that this will actually happen—the packers' clout in national politics is substantial.[8]

A related proposal that has been advanced by Senators Chuck Grassley (R-IA) and Jon Tester (D-MT) is to mandate that more of the fat cattle market be conducted in the negotiated spot market rather than in the unreported market for forward contracts. Over the last three decades, the spot market for fat cattle has diminished to less than 20 percent of all cattle sold, with most of the remaining 80 percent purchased through unpriced "captive supply" arrangements. Because the captive supply cattle prices are ultimately based on the spot market sales, which is subject to manipulation by the packers, Senators Grassley and Tester propose that a minimum of 50 percent of the cattle purchases be done in the negotiated spot market.[9]

The packing cartel argues that there is nothing wrong with the cattle market—it is all just a matter of supply and demand. In a Senate hearing in July 2021, Senator Grassley pointed out that packers were making up to $1,000 per head after owning the cattle for less than two weeks, while cattle producers who had owned the cattle for a year and half were losing money, and consumers were paying more for the beef. According to Senator Grassley, cattle feeders were receiving between $1,500 and $1,700 per head, while packers were selling the beef for $2,500 to $2,700 per head. The actual cost of slaughtering and processing a steer is about $200.[10] This means that packers were clearing $1,300 to $1,500 per head for no reason whatsoever.

The executives from Tyson and JBS who also testified at this hearing explained that this is supply and demand at work. The COVID-19 pandemic sickened many packing plant workers, reducing the packers' capability to slaughter cattle, resulting in a surplus of cattle ready to be processed. Since they were not slaughtering as many cattle, a deficit of beef available for retail translated into higher prices for consumers. But as the packer executives reminded us, it was just a simple matter of supply and demand. Never mind that the packing cartel bottleneck created both the surplus of cattle and the shortage of beef!

The packer executives have a point, albeit a limited one. Supply-and-demand forces legitimately control markets—at least they should. Antitrust laws do not exist to punish business for unethical behavior; there are other laws for that. However, antitrust laws exist to protect competition. When competition becomes compromised, the result is all manner of harm to society and the economy. In the case of this COVID-19 pandemic, what was revealed is that the packing cartel controls a bottleneck easily subject to disruption, with the convenient side effect of being able to price gouge on both ends. If this country had fifty cattle packing companies instead of just four, the bottleneck and resulting price gouging would not have occurred, at least not on the scale that it has. As for the workforce being put at risk of contracting COVID-19, with more packing companies, workers would have a better chance to demand better health and working conditions.

The packer cartel maintains that their size is necessary in order to have optimum "economies of scale." But for whose benefit is this "economy of scale?" Certainly not the producers, workers, nor, ultimately, the consumers. Even their claimed efficiency in processing is questionable, as small packers report to have equal or even better line efficiencies. Economic research shows that there is no "economy of scale" efficiencies beyond operating a single modern plant capable of slaughtering and processing up to 2 percent of the beef or pork in the nation. This means that there could be one hundred competing firms—fifty in hogs and fifty in cattle. It is the cartel's convenient domination over the market that allows them to exploit the land, the animals, the producers, the workforce, and the consumers.

The packers prefer that nothing changes. The bill proposed by Grassley and Tester, which would require that 50 percent of the fat cattle be purchased on the spot market, would be from the packers' perspective a drastic solution. However, the spot market proposal has other legality concerns, because it would dictate how private entities can conduct their business. Inevitably, there would be a lot of pushback from the courts.

Senator Booker's proposal, which would require that all fat cattle be marketed through a competitive, transparent market mechanism, has a stronger legal foundation and would be a better solution. This was how the consent decree that went along with the P&S Act was structured. Simply put, since it worked in 1921, it should work in 2021.

Promoting Competition in the American Economy

On July 9, 2021, President Biden weighed in with a far-reaching executive order called Promoting Competition in the American Economy. The order directs departments and agencies to come up with a range of regulatory changes that would enhance market competition and restore basic fairness in a number of industries. In the case of the USDA, the executive order covers several of the issues already proposed by Senators Booker, Tester, and Grassley. One of them is for the USDA to address the fraudulent use of the "Product of USA" label, a matter discussed earlier in this essay.

The president's orders also include reinstating the GIPSA rules to better define unfair, unjustly discriminatory, and/or deceptive practices in the poultry, pork, and cattle markets. This includes interpreting the P&S Act such that producers do not have to demonstrate industry-wide harm to assert a violation of the act when it was just themselves who have been harmed.

The order also calls for the preparation of a report on the effects of retail concentration and retailers' practices on market competition in the food industries. In further directs that $500 million be spent to promote building and expanding smaller packing plants to compete with the packing cartel.

Finally, the order addresses the issue of "right to repair." By restricting access to the advanced electronic diagnostic and control capabilities of modern farm equipment, the farm equipment cartel forces farmers to have their machinery repaired at the dealerships. The service departments at the dealerships are expensive, while many farmers and independent mechanics are equally capable of repairing a piece of equipment if they had access to the computer that controls the machines functions. Farmers need the right to repair their own machinery.

Biden's executive order puts in motion a whole range of reforms that farmers and livestock producers have been demanding over the past three decades. The problem with executive orders is that the next administration can simply nullify them. This was the case when the Trump administration reversed a whole host of regulations, such as the GIPSA rules put in place by the Obama administration. Hopefully, the regulatory reforms that are proposed in the Promoting Competition in the American Economy order will be supported by farmers once they understand the benefits and will, therefore, survive the next change of administrations.

One issue the president's executive order did not address includes a call from American dairy farmers outlined in a recent press release asking for a Milk from Family Dairies Act. The farmers' argument is that "decentralizing dairy production and fair price standards for producers would bring family-scale dairy farms back to rural communities across the country, along with regional processors and increased economic activity across many sectors. Regional dairy production is more transparent and resilient to shocks. Smaller-scale farms are more likely to graze their cows on grass rather than keeping them in large barns year round. Grazing sequesters carbon, reduces water and air pollution, and is better for overall cow health."[11]

It is insane that we have allowed our milk production to be concentrated into the middle of the vast irrigation districts of California and Idaho while family dairies in the hills and valleys of Wisconsin and New England are going broke. The nation's supply of milk, butter, and cheese is now highly vulnerable to climatic extremes, not to mention earthquakes. These mega-dairies also pose a daily risk of fecal contamination downstream in the irrigation system. Meanwhile, rural communities across the nation vanish as their last family dairy gives up.

Other Agricultural Sectors Requiring Reform

You may have noticed that the above segments were almost exclusively about restoration of fairness and competition in the livestock sector. Little was proposed that would benefit crop farmers. The reason is that over the last three decades, it has been primarily livestock producers who have been vocal in calling for a restoration of market competition. This effort has been led by the cow/calf sector of the cattle industry, which is the last segment of American agriculture that still markets through a transparent public market system. Most other sectors of American agriculture have been subsumed into nontransparent price mechanisms, such that farmers are no longer independent enough to organize for reform.

Crops such as malting barley, sugar beets, and many vegetables are now raised under contract, like the situation faced by poultry and hog producers. There is nothing inherently wrong with producing a crop under contract if the contracting negotiations are open and transparent. But there is the "rub," as Shakespeare would have said.

Contract growers of poultry and hogs can attest that their system has resulted in servitude, and these growers are now seeking redress by calling for stiffer oversight of their parent companies through the P&S Act. Whether that will be successful remains to be seen. But while livestock producers have theoretical protection written into the P&S Act, other sectors of agriculture do not have that much legal protection from abusive behavior on the part of the cartel controlling that segment of agriculture.

The field crop sector, which is a huge portion of agriculture (lumping together corn, soybeans, wheat, barley, rice, oats, cotton, beans, and various oilseed crops) are ultimately all dependent on exports to clear the market of excess production. It is not that all these crops are actually exported in large quantities, but these alternative field crops are, in the end, priced based on the market prices for corn, soybeans, and wheat. Therefore, the export levels of corn, soybeans, and wheat determine the price for all of the others, such that a reduction in exports causes low prices for all field crops. Although the "free traders" who negotiated trade agreements like NAFTA promised that exports would be the path to agricultural prosperity, that has not worked out as well as advertised.

There is nothing wrong with exporting excess food production; however, having our markets dependent on exports is dangerous. It makes our farm economy vulnerable to all manner of disruptions emanating from foreign places. War, climatic instability, economic mismanagement, disruptions in critical supply chains—all their calamities become ours. Farmers are all the more vulnerable because the international markets for the commodities are controlled by the global agro-industrial cartels, which are able to profit regardless of what is disrupting the market.

The central problem with export markets is that they are global and not free. Almost every country except for the United States plans and controls the production of their basic food needs. These countries only buy on the global market when they have a deficit. Since our country's farm policy pretends that the world market is a "free market," it is our farmers who bear the risk and are totally dependent on exports to clear the market at a price that would allow farmers to survive for another year. American farmers are the residual suppliers for a global system that is designed to exploit them. A solution would be for our government to build into our trade agreements guaranteed purchase commitments. Thereby, our production could be managed to better meet the export demand, and farmgate prices would be stabilized.

Overproduction of Corn

As discussed previously, the cancer at the heart of the chronic American farm crisis is this country's ability to overproduce corn. And as discussed, this is a very good problem to have—unless you are a farmer. It is for this reason that American agriculture has become so dependent on exports and gasohol. And here we have a huge problem looming.

Automotive technology is rapidly moving toward electric vehicles. Although the ethanol industry began in the 1970s, ethanol production as a major factor in the corn market is a relatively recent phenomenon dating back just twenty years, when Congress mandated the use of E10 fuel as part of its renewable fuel standard program to reduce greenhouse gas emissions.[12] This increase in demand for corn resulted in higher prices, which prior to 2005 averaged $2.27 per bushel and has since averaged $4.20. The increase in corn prices and demand also resulted in an increase in overall production, from an annual average of 2.4 billion bushels before 2006 to 6.2 billion bushels now. Much of that increased production came from more acres devoted to corn, which before 2007 averaged 79.1 million acres and averages 91.1 million acres now.[13]

The implication of increased oversupply that will result from a decreased demand for gasohol will certainly be a topic in the debate over the next farm bill, which is supposed to have been scheduled for 2023, but because of chronic dysfunction in Congress, a farm bill will most probably not be passed until sometime in 2024. I say debate, but it is usually not much of debate because this is when the big dogs get together to decide and the small dogs (farmers) get told.

But climate change will also be an issue in this coming farm bill. There is a widespread belief that if farming practices were to be improved, agriculture could sequester more carbon in the soil. I am skeptical of the overall practicality and impact of this concept, except in one circumstance. Much of the increased production of corn discussed above comes from center-pivot irrigation pumping from the Ogallala Aquifer that runs beneath Nebraska, through Kansas, Oklahoma, and eastern Colorado, to northern Texas. The Ogallala is a rapidly depleting fossil source of water.

The land above the Ogallala Aquifer was historically the tallgrass prairie, which many characterize as an imperiled ecosystem. A solution would be for the next farm bill to expand the Conservation Reserve Program to convert the irrigated fields of corn that we will not need back to tall-grass prairie. This would satisfy at least three constituencies: hunting and wildlife enthusiasts, those advocating for carbon sequestration in soils, and the farm sector concerned about the price-depressing fact of too much corn on the market. It is not all a win-win situation, however. Higher corn prices and more land put back into rangeland will result in higher livestock feed costs and more cows grazing on the newly restored tall grass prairie. This will result in lower prices for cattle producers and higher chicken, pork, and beef prices at retail. The livestock industry will oppose expanding the Conservation Reserve Program, which would reduce the number of acres planted to corn and soybeans. Farm policy is complicated.

The Direct-to-Consumer Food Markets

When I was studying at the Sorbonne in 1966, one of the "must do" experiences was visiting Les Halles, the food wholesale market—*le ventre de Paris* (the belly of Paris), as Émile Zola called it. Les Halles was a grouping of beautiful steel-and-glass structures built in the 1850s and located in the middle of the business district on the right bank of the Seine, where there had been a market since 1137. Over the centuries, the city had grown to surround and hem it in.

Every night, the fresh produce, meat, cheese, seafood, and flowers that fed and ornamented Paris would arrive at Les Halles, where shop owners, open-air market resellers, and restaurateurs would purchase it for the coming day. Because the market operated only in the very early morning, to visit Les Halles you had to get there at three in the morning. By six, only sanitation workers would be left.

In those days, the metro stopped running from midnight to five in the morning, so if you did not live in the center of Paris and did not have the funds to take a taxi, as was my case, one had to plan to stay up the whole night. In early September, my classmate Holly and I decided to visit Les Halles. This was before the weather in Paris got cold, but it was still brisk at night.

During the weekdays, the bistros in Paris would close by eleven or twelve, so Holly and I had to keep ourselves company for three or four hours before anything would be happening at the market. We spent much of that time talking and huddled together for warmth on the banks of the Seine.

Les Halles in full swing was a busy place. Lines of men carried sides of pork or quarters of beef on their shoulders from the trucks to the wholesale vendors and then to the waiting vans of the butchers or restauranters. It was not a place designed for tourists, and you needed to stay out of the men's way because theirs was serious work. The experience gave me an appreciation for the complexity of supplying quality food sufficient to feed an entire city. Holly and I ended our adventure with a breakfast of onion soup, fresh bread, and red wine—the traditional worker's fare.

In 1969, Les Halles closed and the market moved to Rungis, a large, modern facility south of Paris near Orly Airport. It was no longer possible to continue hosting the world's largest food market in the middle of Paris, where the streets and infrastructure dated from the Middle Ages. Les Halles has since been converted to a large public plaza with a metro hub below. In the level between the metro and the plaza is a shopping mall.

Today 35 percent of France's food is priced and moved through Rungis and the sixteen other wholesale markets located in each of France's major cities. The food is then retailed through local food stores, restaurants, or sold directly to consumers at the open-air markets that operate in every French village, small town, or quartier.

In the United States, according to the USDA, only 0.4 percent of the food is purchased through a farmer-direct-to-consumer market system, while in France it is 35 percent. Why? Part of the answer seems to be because in 1953, France passed a law, Marchés d'Intérêt National (markets of national interest) that protected the farmer-to-wholesale-to-consumer market system. Back in 1953, the United States marketed much of its food through similar wholesale markets located in every major city in America. But American producers and consumers did not value those markets enough to legally protect and support them.

My in-laws, Maggio and Sons, wholesaled fresh vegetables at the Camden Yards market in Baltimore, but the market went into decline when the supermarket chains took over retail grocery. The national-level grocery conglomerates preferred to purchase produce directly through their own, proprietary market system. The old yards are now the home for the Baltimore Orioles baseball franchise.

In the 1950s and '60s, independent mom-and-pop retailers faced extreme competitive pressure from supermarkets. In self-defense, they formed their own centralized food purchasing companies, which, over time, turned into national-level purchasing and distribution concerns. Today much of the food for independent grocers, restaurants, and institution food services come through corporations such as Sysco or US Foods.

In the American food marketing system, price became the determining factor, not quality or freshness. Food varieties were selected to be able to withstand rough handling, long transports, and extended shelf life. This meant that in many cases, the flavor of the food was compromised. Nor did anyone consider the effect on the farms, small towns, and local businesses that had been part of the local farm-to-wholesale-to-consumer food chain. The link between farmers and consumers was broken when the market that had been local or regional became national.

Farmers that had up until then supplied the nearby cities now sell into a system that supplies supermarket chains. The technology and economic pressure forced farmers to switch from raising a diversity of foods to specializing. Because farmers' choice of markets narrowed as a result of the government's cheap food policy, which discriminates against small farms, the number of farms fell precipitously. The end result is that 209,007 farms now supply 78.7 percent of the food.

Reliable statistics on how much food is sold direct to consumers are hard to find. The best I came up with was a 2015 USDA report whose data is based on 2012 statistics.[14] They concluded that it is only 0.4 percent of the food. This report points out, however, some interesting facts. The customers at local farmers' markets are very loyal—small in number but loyal. No surprise. However, the farmers' market consumers do not necessarily have to pay more for what they buy, because food in farmers' markets sells on average for about 39 percent less than what consumers pay in the supermarkets.[15] It is an erroneous assumption that only the rich can afford to buy food at a farmers' market.

It does not seem intuitively reasonable that only 0.4 percent of the food is sold directly to consumers. The problem comes in defining what is direct to consumer and how the USDA can capture that information. Besides farmers' markets, there are many other direct-to-consumer schemes: roadside stands, food basket subscriptions, shares in the farm's production, online sales, direct sales to restaurants, food hubs, and sales through co-ops or small stores. More recent information reports that "local food represents a small (less than 4 percent of total farm sales) but growing share of the US food system."[16] This is an encouraging trend. Local sales in this country are now about 10 percent of the 35 percent experienced in France.

The partisans of the local food movement are passionate and working to reestablish a niche that at one time was the norm. Why, then, is this important? It is not that *all* food should be marketed through a local system, it is that *more* food should be marketed locally because that has tremendous benefits to local communities beyond those of just the individual farmer and the consumer of locally grown food. Resiliency is the first issue that comes to mind. The COVID-19 pandemic hit the meat industry hard. Infections among packing plant workers caused plants to shut down. For a period, in some cities, meat counters were empty. Retail prices increased while producer prices hit bottom. Packer shareholders made a killing, as packing plant workers got killed. As animals in the industrial system got backed up because of closed or slowed packing plants, small, local plants tried to take up some of the slack but were immediately overwhelmed. Many of these small packing plants supply consumers who can buy a whole hog or quarter of beef at a time and have the freezer capacity to store it. These slaughter facilities are not equipped or licensed to sell meal by the piece. Even those that have federal meat inspectors on premise cannot easily access the retail consumers, because there is no market mechanism that allows for small plants to sell to the retail giants. This is by design. The retail and meat-packing cartels do not want the competition.

If we want a resilient food system able to withstand a pandemic or climatic adversity, we need more than just farmers and consumers. There is also a need to restore the entire infrastructure in between. We need big packing plants, but we need numerous smaller local ones too. The small, local plants need access to consumers at supermarkets. The more market channels there are, the more transparently competitive the market would be, and the more resilient the food system would become.

We also need to restore the central role of land-grant universities in agricultural research. In choosing to not adequately fund our university agricultural scientists, our society has left the door open for global agri-cartels to take control of the technology of agriculture. As a result, firms like Bayer and Syngenta dominate seed technology as well as the sale and development of herbicides and livestock pharmaceuticals.

These corporations are poised to control access to the next important agricultural innovation: "precision ag," which promises to better target fertilizer, herbicide, and pesticide applications. This is not at all necessary, because the most important information for "precision ag" comes from technology that the taxpayers have already paid for—satellites. "Precision ag" technology needs to be open source and available to all farmers in the world, not just those tied to and controlled by the global agri-cartels.

The central problem in agriculture is the domination by a small number of firms that control both the critical inputs and purchase the resulting production. Although the advent of these cartels predates the *Citizens United* decision of 2010, when the Supreme Court ruled that corporations could spend unlimited amounts to influence elections, this ruling makes antitrust enforcement that much more difficult. There is a proposed amendment to the Constitution, the Democracy for All Amendment, that is languishing in our divided Congress, which would ban corporations from buying elections.[17] Polling shows that most Americans, Republicans and Democrats alike, support such an amendment. It is our political dysfunction that prevents passage.

The Not COOL Story

For those of us who advocate for reform in agricultural policy, 2021 was a heady year. Much of what has been advanced for reform over the decades is actually on the table; it is actually being considered; it may even become national policy. However, as of 2023, none are yet real, and the opposition is just now rolling out their big guns.

The story of COOL is a sobering one: just when proponents thought it was in the bag, COOL was snatched away. Country of Origin Labeling for beef and pork was made law in 2002 and repealed thirteen years later. During that period, COOL was only fully implemented for two years.

Prior to 1994, before NAFTA and subsequent trade agreements were ratified, there were minimal food imports into the United States, making the labeling of food with country of origin essentially a nonissue. In contrast, imported manufactured items (but not food) were required to be labeled since the passage of the Tariff Act of 1930.

Following the implementation of NAFTA, food imports, particularly imported beef, began to impact the market. Cattle producers sued Canada for dumping subsidized cattle into our market, and proved their case. However, our government refused to sanction Canada. Producers then demanded that imported beef be labeled. The thinking was that if consumers knew the true origin, they would choose beef born and raised in the United States.

In 2002, mandatory labeling of beef, pork, poultry, seafood, fruit, and vegetables was passed. The Bush administration refused to implement it. COOL was once again mandated within the 2008 farm bill, and the Obama administration proceeded to write the regulations for implementation.

But opposition to COOL was led by the North American Meat Institute (NAMI), the Canadian Cattle Association (CCA), and the National Cattlemen's Beef Association (NCBA). They argued that COOL provided no benefit to consumers, who, in any case, did not want it, and that implementation would be enormously expensive, a cost that would be deducted from the price of cattle.

When polled, 86 percent of consumers say that they would appreciate knowing the origin of their beef, which clearly means that COOL would, in fact, benefit US producers.[18] The first two of the anti-COOL coalition's allegations were simply not true. As for the third assertion that implementation was expensive, it was easily shown that the cost assumptions used by the opponents to COOL were ridiculously inflated. Actual costs, once COOL was implemented, proved to be a fraction of a penny per pound.

However, the anti-COOL trio did not give up on their campaign to prevent COOL, and they sued—and eventually lost—in federal courts. Dr. Sally J. Herrin, in an analysis of the anti-COOL legal arguments, wrote:

> The NCBA alleges in its lawsuit that the final 2013 COOL rule violates the constitutionally protected rights to freedom of speech for meatpackers, and that COOL labels provide "no benefit" to consumers.
>
> In other words, the NCBA is claiming that meatpackers have a First Amendment right to deceive consumers.[19]

COOL was finally fully implemented in 2013, but by then a WTO tribunal had ruled on the trade complaint brought by the governments of Canada and Mexico that COOL violated the terms of NAFTA. The chair of this tribunal had been a trade official for the government of

Mexico. None of the livestock or citizens' organizations who favored COOL were allowed to address the tribunal.[20]

In 2015, after only two years of full implementation, the Republican majority in Congress repealed COOL for beef and pork. Other covered commodities, including lamb, poultry, seafood, fruits, and vegetables, continue to be labeled. The immediate effect was that the market for cattle collapsed by 40 percent and stayed at that below-cost-of-production level for the next six years. I bring up this rather tedious history to inform the reader of how fierce the fight for agricultural policy inevitably is. Even COOL, something essentially neutral and obviously beneficial to both consumers and producers, triggers a fight to the death from the global agri-cartels.

The political division between those opposing and advocating for COOL is not exactly what we commonly think of in terms of right versus left, or even Republican versus Democrat. Instead, the division is corporate versus farmers. The organizations allied to oppose COOL and those in favor clearly exhibit that division.

NAMI bills itself as the "one unified voice for meat and poultry companies, large and small."[21] Obviously, the four companies dominating beef-packing had much to gain from rescinding COOL, because they own packing plants all around the globe. The small packing companies that NAMI also claims to represent—not so much. If anything, the small companies in NAMI had as much to lose as cattle ranchers and feeders did.

The CCA website says that it is the national voice of Canada's 60,000 beef farms and feedlots. One can understand how Canadian cattle producers would believe that they were protecting their economic interests, even though it was hypocritical, because Canada has its own COOL law. The CCA victory over COOL resulted in lower cattle prices for Canadian beef, because the actual priority for their partner NAMI was to import beef from South America and Australia, not Canada. Their victory over COOL allowed the beef cartel to import beef with impunity, collapsing cattle prices in Mexico and Canada just as much as it has in the United States.

Of this anti-COOL trio, the most perplexing is the NCBA.

According to their website, the NCBA was "initiated in 1898, . . . [and] is the marketing organization and trade association for America's one million cattle farmers and ranchers. . . . NCBA is a consumer-focused, producer-directed organization representing the largest segment of the nation's food and fiber industry."[22] First off, according to the USDA, there are only 779,386 cattle producers and ranchers in the United States, not a million. There were well over 1 million not that long ago, which shows that the NCBA website manager is not keeping current with the consequences of the NCBA's advocacy for policies benefiting the global beef cartel. Out of 779,386 engaged in raising cattle, only about 30,000 are actual NCBA members.[23] In most cafés and bars where Montana ranchers gather, if asked what they think of the NCBA, the response would be too crude to print. Clearly, the NCBA does not represent America's *1 million* cattle farmers and ranchers as it has claimed.

In a community where most cattlemen vote conservative, you would think that NCBA membership would be common. And in every gathering of ranchers, there are always a few who are members, although they are not too vocal in acknowledging that fact. Membership in the NCBA is the portal to acceptance within the inner circles of the Republican Party, which explains the NCBA's clout and their opposing views on COOL.

Every commodity has its own industry organization similar in power, and with a pro-corporate agenda, to the NCBA. These commodity organizations claim to represent the entire industry but generally oppose any policies that would reform industry practices, increase market competition, and threaten the hegemony of the firms that control that particular commodity. The global agri-cartels fund and cultivate these commodity organizations to be the public face for policies that benefits themselves. The cartels themselves rarely take a public stance. Having ranchers and farmers as their public voices gives these corporations a sort of grassroots legitimacy.

In the case of the NCBA, the bulk of their funding comes not from membership dues but from a dollar-a-head tax that all cattle producers are required to pay each time a cow changes ownership.

Yearly, about $85 million is raised by this tax, which by statute is to be used to promote the consumption of beef. Half is allocated by the state organization authorized to collect it. The other half, $43 million, goes to a USDA-organized board that is controlled by the NCBA. This board, in turn, grants most of the monies to the NCBA to fund beef promotional campaigns.[24] The tax funds (commonly referred to as the checkoff) pays for ads such as "Beef! It's what's for dinner."

It is in the administration of the checkoff funds that the NCBA can leverage the tax monies to fund their advocacy for antiproducer policies. Their senior staff is paid from both checkoff and non-checkoff sources, confusing what is policy advocacy and what is beef promotion.[25] In other words, the 749,386 producers who are not members of the NCBA are required by law to pay a tax that is used to advocate for policies that are detrimental to their interests.

The American Farm Bureau Federation (AFBF) is another player in the pro-corporate network of organizations. According to their website, "The American Farm Bureau Federation is the Voice of Agriculture®. We are farm and ranch families working together to build a sustainable future of safe and abundant food, fiber and renewable fuel for our nation and the world."[26] The AFBF is, in actuality, an insurance company with policies closely aligned with the U.S. Chamber of Commerce. The AFBF did not take a direct public position on COOL. Sometimes their official policies, which are set by the members in the individual state affiliates—who often have libertarian views—are at odds with what the national bosses would wish. When this happens, the AFBF works behind the scenes advocating for the corporations, and their members never know the difference.

The organizations that advocate in favor of family agriculture are more fragmented and less well financed. The largest, and the only one with its own income source, is the National Farmers Union (NFU), whose vision is "a world in which farm families and their communities are respected, valued, and enjoy economic prosperity and social justice" and whose mission is to "advocate for family farmers and their communities through education, cooperation, and legislation."[27] The NFU, like the AFBF, is mostly independently financed through its insurance, fuel refineries, gas stations, and other cooperative endeavors. Unlike the AFBF, the NFU does not claim everyone who does business with them as being a member or an actual farmer.

Other groups advocating on the pro–family farmer side tend to be regional and/or issue oriented. For instance, there are organizations that represent organic or natural farmers, organizations for different field crops, fruit producers, family dairy farms, contract poultry producers, and cattle ranchers. Others in this diffuse coalition are more consumer oriented, or environmental, or motivated by issues of social justice, including the principals of market competition. All suffer from underfunding and are, therefore, jealous of one another because they attract many of the same members and tap the same funding sources.

Too many of these more progressive anti-corporate organizations are clones of one another, forming after schisms caused by leaders who broke with the parent organization over personality differences. This was the case in the United States Cattlemen's Association, which split from Ranchers-Cattlemen Action Legal Fund United Stockgrowers of America. Both have essentially the same advocacy agenda, and both oppose the pro-corporate policies of the NCBA. Together their membership exceeds that of the NCBA, but hard feelings prevent close collaboration.

I bring all this up not to dispirit everyone, but to make clear how complicated debates over ag policy inevitably are. The easy out for any senator or representative is to say that their hands are tied because the industry is not united. Often this is a convenient excuse because the money that the ag chemical, pharmaceutical, seed, farm machinery, grain, meat-packer, and retail giants—not to mention big banks—donate has more influence with many in Congress than do the 2 million farmers whose votes are easily divided by hot-button cultural issues. However, there are about 330 million consumers of food in America, and their opinions do cause policymakers to stop and consider. If consumers favor producing food on farms owned by family farmers, the debate on agricultural policy would have very different outcomes. As it stands, the farmers who raise the food are the least influential segment of the huge industry that feeds America.

According to the USDA, in 2019, the food industry amounted to $1.1 trillion dollars—5.2 percent of the total GDP, employing nearly 19.7 percent of the total workforce, most of whom work in restaurants, retail stores, and processing. The actual producers of the food, including farm labor, account for only 2.6 million of that number. The farm sector receives only 12 percent ($136 billion) of the total $1.1 trillion generated.[28] You can readily see that when 5.2 percent of the GDP employs 19.7 percent of the workforce, the food industry is based on underpaying for labor—including the labor of farmers.

For most consumers, the fact that food is cheap would be seen as a positive until they consider that the entire industry is so precariously balanced, it may as well be resting on the head of a pin. As we have previously discussed, 209,007 farms produce 78.7 percent of the food. They in turn sell to about 25 firms, which process, transform, and ultimately retail that food to 330 million consumers. These dominant firms exploit an underpaid workforce that comprises one in five working Americans. This is an absurdly vulnerable system on which we rely to put food on our tables. It is even more vulnerable under conditions where the world is heating up, causing the climate to go crazy and disrupting food production, which, in turn, results in massive movements of refugees fleeing civil war and collapsing economies.

As this essay demonstrates, the cartels that control food are well entrenched and will not voluntarily give up their control. However, they are vulnerable because they are all in violation of the principles of free enterprise. At its core, agricultural reform is about trust-busting and reestablishing transparent, competitive markets for food raised on farms that are owned and managed by real farmers. It is clear what needs doing, but it will take support from the people who eat the food to get it done.

Bridging the Rural-Urban Divide

And just as, from the fold, come sheep—
first one, then two, then three, the flock
stand meek, and faces earthward keep,

and if one walks, the rest will walk:
and when he stops, huddle in place,
meek, mild, not knowing why they balk.
    —Dante Alighieri, *Purgatory* (translated by A. E. Stallings)

By August 2021, three million acres of the American West had burned, well in advance of when we typically expect wildfires. This drought is the worst that I have experienced on my ranch. The full extent of the drought is huge, stretching from North Dakota to Texas and all the way west to the Pacific—a full one-third of the continental United States. In 2022, the water level in Lake Mead on the Colorado River was the lowest ever. Water rationing in Arizona and Nevada is sure to come.

Meanwhile, hundreds of people were swept away in a flash flood in Germany. On the opposite side of the world in Japan, another flash flood drowned passengers in a subway train. As for my ranch, the hay harvest is less than half of what we need for the winter. Where the necessary feed can be bought is an open question because everyone is experiencing the same disaster. The government will probably be giving us emergency drought payments, but you can't buy hay that does not exist.

Is this climate change or just a climatic anomaly? Should the cattle and sheep be culled to adjust for a new normal, or will it rain this coming spring? If we decide to turn the mother cows into hamburger, there will be no replacements to be purchased next year, because we will have eaten the factory. The future, in this case, will bring higher beef prices for consumers and less income for ranchers. The alternative is to buy exorbitantly high-priced feed from far away. One might be able to limp through the winter, saving the herd for at least this coming year. For myself and my neighbors, there is no correct decision; it is a flip of the coin and time will tell if it was right or wrong.

Wild swings and extremes in weather are increasingly looking to be the new reality. Inevitably, uncertainty in food supply chains will also be the new reality. Can our industrial, centrally controlled system of agriculture, on which we currently rely, meet the challenge of supplying our food needs under these adverse conditions? If industrial agriculture cannot, is it too late to transition to a more diversified and flexible form of agriculture that would be more resilient? These are questions that we should study, but will we? Judging from our nation's track record over the past two decades—beginning with the attack on the Twin Towers on September 11, 2001; the economic meltdown of 2008; and the COVID-19 pandemic that started in 2020—Americans appear to be irreconcilably divided, no longer capable of rationally resolving existential questions.

In this political environment, the rural-urban divide has become even more extreme. In this past session, the Montana Legislature stripped the authority from the county health officers because the officials were restricting taverns from operating as they wished during a global pandemic.[1] On a roll, the legislature then voted to allow college students to go armed on campus and drunks to carry six-shooters in bars.[2] It is unclear what Bat Masterson and Wyatt Earp, sheriffs in the Old West, would have said about gun-toting college students, but they would have certainly warned that arming drunks is a bad idea. Flush with those victories, the legislature went on to deny children struggling with their gender identity the right to play on the school basketball team.[3] Talk about solving a nonproblem with just plain meanness.

On July 6, 2021, a woman who was biking across Montana was dragged from her tent and killed by a grizzly bear in the small town of Ovando. Had she been in the middle of the Bob Marshall Wilderness, one might say that she should have been prepared for the risk. But this attack happened in a small town just off a major highway in the town park next to the post office. Earlier in May 2021, a grizzly traveled two hundred miles to the Snowy Mountains, where it killed some cattle. Another thirty miles to my place for lamb would not have been much of a jaunt. The predator-control agents controlled that bear, and my sheep remain safe until the next bear ventures in this direction, or I must sell them because of prolonged drought—whichever comes first.

What the one side sees as a heroic stand to save the planet by saving the bears, the other sees as a deliberate assault on their livelihoods, communities, and culture. In the summer of 2021, the coronavirus made a resurgence because rural Americans refused to be vaccinated just because a president from the other party tells them they should. They created a pandemic of the unvaccinated, killing only themselves. Why people who routinely vaccinate their livestock refuse to protect themselves has no answer. It is like a theater of the absurd. Political scientists and psychologists will have to battle that out, because I, for one, cannot explain.

In the preface to these essays, I wrote about Frank and Deborah Popper, professors from Rutgers University who advocated for the restoration of bison on the North American Great Plains. The message received by the human inhabitants of the Great Plains is that bison are more important than we who currently live, work, and love this land.

In the thirty years following the Poppers' recommendations, the assault on rural America and rural Americans has intensified. The Buffalo Commons is becoming a reality, not covering multiple states as originally envisioned by the Poppers but sizable nonetheless. The American Prairie Reserve (APR) is doing the best they can manage in their mission to *rewild* the Great Plains, and the BLM allowed the APR to put bison on 63,500 acres of public lands,[4] with no consideration given to the impact on the neighboring ranches.

Rich people have always had the option to buy a place in the country, but given the accumulation of wealth by the 1 percent, rural Montana now has a surfeit of ultrawealthy landowners. They have become a dominant presence on our landscape but generally not in our communities, because most don't bother to live among us. The few who do, however, come to believe that they are entitled to run the place. Witness Montana's current governor Greg Gianforte and Representative Matt Rosendale, transplants from New Jersey and Maryland, respectively. Meanwhile, advocates for wild animals continue to proliferate and their campaigns are bearing fruit. Grizzly bears are now a serious public danger.

The pandemic caused supply chains to lurch to a halt, revealing the central weakness in the much-vaunted global manufacturing just-in-time-delivery system. The first casualty, besides toilet paper, was N95 face masks. It turns out that this country hardly manufactures them anymore and many of the face masks hastily ordered from China were more suited for use as toilet paper. Doctors and nurses were forced to make their own.

COVID-19 infected the workers in the packing plants, causing closures and reductions in capacity. For a time, meat cases were bare, while beef prices went up. Then in June 2021, JBS, one of the world's largest food companies, was shut down for a week by Russian ransom hackers. In one fell swoop, our country lost 23 percent of its beef-, 18 percent of its pork-, and 17 percent of its chicken-processing capacity.[5] The COVID-19 pandemic revealed more than just our vulnerability in meat-packing. Our economy is vulnerable to disruption in a great many sectors. For instance, too many vital pharmaceuticals and medical supplies are no longer manufactured in this country. We are just now waking up to the realization that most of the microchips for the world are manufactured in Taiwan, an island claimed by China, which they might invade at any moment.

As our economy recovers from the effects of the pandemic, there were not enough truck drivers to distribute goods waiting to be unloaded from container ships off the coast of Los Angeles. At Christmas, many children may have had to do without their most desired toy. Perhaps this in itself is not so bad, but many important parts crucial to restarting the economy were also floating in container ship limbo. We created these vulnerabilities by the policies that we, as a citizenry, have both made and not made.

The Montana Democratic Party lost in a landslide in the 2022 election. Historically, Montana has been evenly divided between red and blue, so something changed. To find out what, the Democrats sent out a questionnaire to sympathetic rural voters. The conclusion was that the Democratic candidates need to be more sensitive to rural economic issues such as health care, access to broadband internet, funding for schools, and agricultural policy. In short, they concluded that no change was needed even though the Montana Democratic platform was clearly not resonating with voters. For instance, their survey did not consider that grizzly bears, bison, wolves, feral horses, prairie dogs, sage grouse, or wildfires could have played a role in the election. Anger at the imposition of wildlife by outside forces should not be sufficient reason for the rural-urban political division to swing so many voters to the extremes, but rationality does not outweigh emotional responses.

Global Warming Is Happening Faster Than Predicted

Recently, the news on the radio was about a United Nations report concluding that global warming is happening faster than previously predicted.[6] Climate scientists believe that even more extreme climatic weather phenomena is to come, and they are calling for faster conversion from burning fossil fuels. This is sensible, as we should prioritize prevention. But so far there has not been much public debate on how we can live with climate change, because chances are we will not be successful in a complete reversal. Obviously, or at least it should be obvious, one thing we should worry about is our ability to produce food under adverse growing conditions.

The fact that 209,007 farms produce 78.7 percent of the food while 1,820,192 farms produce the remaining 21.3 percent should be an area of concern, and defines the root causes for the division between rural and urban America. The 209,007 farms that produce raw materials for global agro-industry are not numerous or profitable enough to sustain the infrastructure needed to have robust rural communities. The services and activities that make a community an economically viable and pleasant place to live have disappeared because the money that is being produced from the land is sucked out to enrich big, international agribusiness.

The 1,820,192 small family farmers depend on off-farm employment as their primary income source. But most off-farm jobs in rural areas are minimum wage. According to the USDA, in 2019, rural poverty levels are 15.8 percent, in contrast to 11.9 percent in metropolitan areas.[7] There is simply too little money flowing through the rural economy.

Family farms have two choices. They can market into the international agribusiness system, which does not really want to bother with small-scale production and, therefore, discriminates against these small farmers, or family farmers can sell direct to consumers as best they can. However, because the direct-to-consumer infrastructure is inadequate in most parts of the country, it is an inefficient and expensive way to market food.

Global agro-industry sucks the profits out of rural places all around the world, leaving farming populations impoverished and resentful. In poorer countries, this results in mass economic migration. In this country, it factors into polarization and political dysfunction.

Dante's Sheep

We are living through mind-blowing, complicated times. Divisive, confusing times! For twenty years, this country won every battle in Afghanistan yet spectacularly lost the war. Cutting-edge, hi-tech warfare was defeated by obstinacy. Our enlightened liberal beliefs about democracy and the dignity of men and women have been thrown back in our faces.

The forces of obstinacy in this country are questioning the shared and presumed universal values of democracy and cultural inclusion. Political norms have been shattered. The veneer of civil discourse has been ripped off, showing nothing but ugliness beneath. Like Dante's sheep, we are bewildered as we exit the familiar fold. We balk, not knowing which way to turn. We are forced to reassess our future as a united people, as a welcoming culture, even as a democracy. Without an honest assessment and clear resolve, it is not guaranteed that this country shall survive as the United States of America we have long presumed it to be.

The rural-urban divide is a prominent feature of this cultural and political dysfunction. As climatic instability increasingly stresses our and the world's ability to feed itself, more confusion and anger is inevitable. How shall it be addressed? Many, in this country and across the world, are looking toward authoritarianism. There is a worldwide resurgence of fascism, infecting countries that we had safely numbered among the democracies, but also here, at home, within our ranks.

A century ago, fascism was the political response that falsely promised to contain the misery of a worldwide economic collapse, a depression created by the excesses of capitalism. The capitalists, fearing that they were losing control to the movement demanding rights for working-class people, supported demagogues. Are the global capitalists again joining forces with unprincipled sociopaths to maintain their riches and prerogatives? Clearly some are systematically funding the extremist right. Thankfully, it is not certain that all the capitalists agree on an overthrow of democracy.

It is wrong to focus just on the negative, because the majority of Americans are not willing to concede the future to fascism. People are pushing back with movements such as Black Lives Matter and #MeToo. Across the globe, people are debating the issues that divide us and they are also pushing back against the ugliness. It is, however, a confusing debate, as any honest debate must be. We each approach the podium from our own parochial interests: from the limitations that our experiences, education, and prejudices allow—for none of us are omniscient. But debate we must if we are to survive.

Completely mitigating the coming disruptions in food production is probably not possible. We are already witnessing famine, famine-encouraged war, and famine-induced economic migration. The Syrian civil war was triggered by the worst drought that the Levant had experienced in the last nine hundred years.[8]

The drought-induced economic crisis in Syria led to a demand for a more responsive and inclusive government. The demonstrations for democracy were met with suppression, torture, murder, and destruction, forcing a mass migration that made its desperate way through Turkey and Greece and on to mainland Europe. We attempted to address the tragedy of Syria through military means, but as we experienced in Afghanistan, soldiers are incapable of solving complex economic and ecological issues.

In response to our military intervention, terrorists and jihadists flocked to Syria to confront "the Great Satan," (a phrase coined by former Iranian leader Ayatollah Ruhollah Khomeini to describe the United States). The caliphate of the Islamic State was ultimately repulsed, but their members found refuge in other failing states, enlisting in other insurgencies. What has been accomplished by our initial folly of waging war on Iraq and Afghanistan and then in Syria has been more failed states, more opportunity for dictators, more loci of jihadism, and millions of hopeless economic migrants.

Changes in climate and the resultant disruptions in food production cannot be stopped at our borders, as demonstrated by the hundreds of thousands of Guatemalans and Haitians massing along the Rio Grande. This economic migration, too, is the direct result of corrupt government, environmental degradation, and drought. It is for these reasons that we must reassess many of the things we have been taking for granted, including whether the current structure of agriculture will be able to meet ours and the rest of humanity's needs.

Centralized planning by the executives of global agro-industry, who now control vast acreages of monocrops, factories full of chickens and pigs, feedlots with hundreds of thousands of steers, dairies with thousands of head of defecating cows, and irrigation systems sucking more water that what naturally falls, is not sustainable. It has already proven it is not sustainable and will be even less so under conditions of more severe weather. If we are to mitigate the effects of climatic instability, we need production diversification such that food is raised on farms owned and managed by real farmers, not global corporations. In addition, we need the proliferation and localization of markets, which result in actual competitive pricing and the shortening of food supply chains.

People have lost faith in markets as a mechanism to organize economic well-being. In large part, this is because what was once the ideal of free enterprise has devolved into crony capitalism and global cartels. The central lie in the neoliberal doctrine is that markets function efficiently if business is left to its own devices, that the invisible hand will provide for us all. The truth is that each industrial sector has its own inherent market dynamic and limitations. Some can function efficiently with minimum oversight while other sectors only benefit society when carefully regulated. Without ground rules and limits, all economic sectors inevitably result in monopolistic cartels.

Retail is most amenable to operating under free-market competitive forces. What needs to be avoided is retail giants dividing up territory, creating localized monopolies. In contrast, from the very beginning of the technology, we understood that electrical generation and distribution, along with communication services, was not adequately subject to competitive market forces. If everyone in the nation was to be served at a reasonable price, utilities had to be regulated. That is why public service commissions were created.

However, in the 1990s, this nation bought the lie of deregulating electricity, communications, and broadcasting hook, line, and sinker. We are paying for that folly in exorbitant electrical bills, crazily expensive and haphazard mobile phone service, and a blackout on independent local news. As for health care, this country is apparently the only one in the world that continues to suffer under the delusion that medical services are subject to supply-and-demand market forces. This costs Americans hundreds of billions of dollars, with tens of millions of people poorly served and hundreds of thousands of lives lost.

Agriculture as an industry is in an in-between situation. Supply-and-demand market forces are crucial to regulate communication between consumers and farmers. But because there are inevitably large numbers of farmers selling to a small number of processors and retailers, the farmers are at a natural negotiation disadvantage.

This is why government intervention to ensure that markets are fair and competitive is an essential feature of agriculture.

In addition, because farming works on an annual cycle, it is difficult for farmers to adjust to changing market demands. To mitigate losses, the individual farmer's rational response to low prices is to raise more of the crop. This results in more product on the market, depressing prices even further. It is for this reason that farmgate prices are always at or below break-even levels. People may question the necessity of farm subsidies and disaster payments, but these are unavoidable costs for having food available every day of the year.

Building That Bridge

It all comes down to food. We delude ourselves if we believe that our economy is based on technology, or manufacturing, or services, or international finance. The very second the grocery store shelves are bare, all these delusions crash. Urban America needs to consider if this country can continue with two separate economic systems—one for the urban and another for the rural—for that is the crux of the matter. Throughout this book, I have written about the cultural issues and the specifics that divide the rural from the urban.

We scream at each other across this chasm of incomprehension. Each time another deranged boy shoots up a school, killing his classmates, urban America rails against gun fanatics frozen in their rhetoric about the sanctity of the Second Amendment. Meanwhile, grizzly bears prowl backyards and farmsteads, yet the Sierra Club sues to prevent their control.

You will probably not find many National Rifle Association members in downtown San Francisco, and by the same token, I would be surprised if there is even one Sierra Club member in Grass Range, Montana. This is as wide a cultural divide as they come, with very poor soil in which to dig abutments for a bridge.

If the issues at stake were not becoming existential, we could perhaps muddle along, just as the distrust between the rural and urban has muddled along since the beginning of the codependency of agriculture and cities. This is not to make light of the rural-urban issues of the past, because entire civilizations disappeared when their agriculture failed. Leaving their homes and temples behind, people suffered, died, or found somewhere to start over. But the coming crisis threatens to be global in its impact. There will be nowhere to run.

We tend to think about climate change as a technical issue, a problem with engineering solutions. And, by some instinct, we avoid the cultural and political dimensions. Perhaps this is because we sense that people in crisis are not rational. We fear their response. The net result so far is that we are barely embracing commonsense technical solutions because of cultural and political dysfunction. Too many are lashing out in denial and putting their faith instead in grifters, charlatans, and sociopaths.

Both sides of this divide need to tone down the rhetoric and reflect on what will actually advance their interests—our common interests. However, the two sides of this divide are not equally powerful. Urban centers are infinitely wealthier and more numerous. Rural America controls just two things: food and consensus. The urban can ignore consensus, confiscate the food, and command the production of more. The global agri-cartels will be happy to comply. But these cartels are part of the problem—in many ways the cause of the problems. It is doubtful that with the cartels in charge, this country, this world, will be able to produce the food to feed a hungry planet.

So, what can urban America do to improve their chances of survival under difficult climatic circumstances? For it is urban Americans who are in control of the dialogue, even if the voting camps appear equally divided. Respect for rural values and knowledge wouldn't hurt. We now have multiple generations raised on the pablum of revisionist fairy tales, where Little Red Riding Hood and the three little pigs go dancing off, arm in arm, with the big bad wolf who, as it turns out, is not so bad a wolf after all. For anyone who has spent a lifetime protecting their sheep and cattle from predators, the wolf-as-your-friend fairy tale does not sit very well.

Urban America, the food-consuming part of America, needs to question if global agro-industry can actually serve its needs. Is the political dysfunction caused by the "cheap food" policy worth it? Will 209,007 farms continue to be capable of producing food as climatic extremes increasingly disrupt agriculture? And is it wise for urban America to continue treating the rural parts of this country as a mere colony?

Will returning to a diversified form of agriculture, enhancing local food markets, encouraging respect for rural sensibilities, and promoting overall economic justice erase the rural-urban divide? Probably not completely, but it might tame some of the craziness. It might allow for the first spans of a bridge to be laid. It might ensure that in the future, we all can eat.

ACKNOWLEDGMENTS

Naturally, everyone whom I have met, interacted with both professionally and socially, and most definitely those with whom I have been the most intimate, helped shape my thinking for this book. However, I will limit these acknowledgments to those who have most influenced my development as an author.

This includes Wilbur and Elizabeth Wood, who have, for the past thirty years, led the Red Truck Writers. This group has met regularly to share and review our writing endeavors. The core of the Red Truck Writers includes Tomi Algers, Tom Thakery, Caroline Pinet, and Fred Longan. All are gifted writers and have helped me focus. Thank you.

In addition, Linda Grosskopf, former editor of the *Western Ag Reporter*, who published a number of my op-eds, volunteered to edit some of my essays, and encouraged me to keep writing. Tess Fahlgren, wife of my stepson Matt Austin, edited and recommended reorganization of the essays in this book. Her input was invaluable. And, finally, I want to thank Baker H. Morrow, editor of this book. Baker and I met as Peace Corps volunteers in Somalia, where we shared a number of adventures and started to grow up.

Finally, I invite readers so inclined to visit my website www.gillestockton.com, where I have posted essays and op-eds I have written through the years, which were germane to my decision to write this book. If it works out, I intend to also post new articles that I hope to write in the future.

NOTES

Preface

1. For those interested in these paintings, see James Keyser, David A. Kaiser, and George R. Poetschat, *Fraternity of War: Plains Indian Rock Art at Bear Gulch and Atherton Canyon, Montana* (Portland: Oregon Archaeological Society Press, 2012).
2. Stephen Ambrose, *Undaunted Courage: Meriwether Lewis, Thomas Jefferson, and the Opening of the American West* (New York: Simon and Schuster, 1996).
3. Elanor Banks, *Wandersong* (Caldwell, ID: Caxton Printers, 1950).
4. See Michelle Lindsey, "The Railroads and the Homesteaders," Homestead on the Range, August 19, 2014, https://homesteadontherange.com/2014/08/19/the-railroads-and-the-homesteaders/.
5. Grass Range History Committee, *From the Foothills to the Plains* (Lewistown, MT: News-Argus Printing, 1999).
6. Anne Matthews, "The Poppers and the Plains," *New York Times Magazine*, June 24, 1990, https://www.nytimes.com/1990/06/24/magazine/the-poppers-and-the-plains.html.

Introduction

1. USDA, National Agricultural Statistics Service, *Agricultural Statistics 2019* (Washington, DC: United States Government Printing Office, 2019), https://downloads.usda.library.cornell.edu/usda-esmis/files/j3860694x/ft849j281/vx022816w/Ag_Stats_2019_Complete_Publication.pdf.
2. James C. Scott, *Against the Grain: A Deep History of the Earliest Agrarian States* (New Haven, CT: Yale University Press, 2017).

3. Ahmed A. Arif, Oluwaseun Adeyemi, Sarah B. Laditka, James N. Laditka, and Tyrone Borders, "Suicide Mortality Rate in Farm-Related Occupations and the Agriculture Industry in the United States," *American Journal of Industrialized Medicine* 64, no. 11 (November 2021): 960–68, https://doi.org/10.1002/ajim.23287.

4. Stacy Mosel, "Substance Abuse in Rural Communities & Small Towns," American Addiction Centers, last modified August 22, 2023, https://americanaddictioncenters.org/rehab-guide/rural-small-town.

5. "Fear Strangers, Trust Scars: Parenting in Papua New Guinea," interview of Jared Diamond by Steve Paulson on *To the Best of Our Knowledge*, April 14, 2018, produced by Steve Paulson, radio show, 11:30, https://www.ttbook.org/interview/fear-strangers-trust-scars-parenting-papua-new-guinea. Diamond said, "They don't tolerate strangers. In a traditional society where people don't move around—where you spend your life in the area where you were born, unless you move to get married—any stranger is usually there for a bad reason—to scout out your territory for a raid or to abduct a woman or to steal a pig. So if you encounter strangers, it's bad."

Once Upon a Time, Old MacDonald Had a Farm

1. USDA, *Agricultural Statistics 2019*.
2. USDA, *Agricultural Statistics 2019*.
3. USDA, *Agricultural Statistics 2019*.
4. Purdue University, Center for Commercial Agriculture, *2019 Indiana Farm Custom Rates*, June 2019, https://ag.purdue.edu/commercialag/home/resource/2019/06/2019-indiana-farm-custom-rates/.
5. Carmen Reinicke, "56% of Americans Can't Cover a $1,000 Emergency Expense with Savings," CNBC, January 19, 2022, https://www.cnbc.com/2022/01/19/56percent-of-americans-cant-cover-a-1000-emergency-expense-with-savings.html.
6. USDA, Economic Research Service, "Farms, Land in Farms, and Average Acres per Farm, 1850–2022," chart, last modified March 14, 2023, https://www.ers.usda.gov/data-products/chart-gallery/gallery/chart-detail/?chartId=58268.
7. Harwood D. Schaffer and Daryll E. Ray, "Recovering US Share of World Crop Exports Is Ag Policy's Zombie Idea," *Policy Pennings*, Agricultural Policy Analysis Center, University of Tennessee, 2020, https://www.agpolicy.org/weekcol/2020/1039.html.
8. *Encyclopaedia Britannica Online*, "neoliberalism," last modified October 8, 2023, https://www.britannica.com/money/topic/neoliberalism.

9. Barry C. Lynn, *Liberty from All Masters: The New American Autocracy vs. The Will of the People* (New York: St. Martin's Press, 2020).

10. Brian Schwartz, "Wall Street Spent over $74 Million to Back Joe Biden's Run for President, Topping Trump's Haul," CNBC, October 28, 2020, https://www.cnbc.com/2020/10/28/wall-street-spends-74-million-to-support-joe-biden.html.

11. Congressional Budget Office, "The Distribution of Household Income, 2019," November 2022, https://www.cbo.gov/publication/58781.

12. Mary K. Hendrickson, Philip H. Howard, Emily M. Miller, and Douglas H. Constance, *The Food System: Concentration and Its Impacts; A Special Report to the Family Farm Action Alliance*, September 14, 2020, https://rules.house.gov/sites/republicans.rules118.house.gov/files/Concentration%20and%20Options%202020%20Final%209%2015.pdf.

13. Hendrickson et al., *Food System*.

14. Benny Bunting, remarks at Northern Plains Council Annual Meeting, 1987.

15. National Chicken Council, "Broiler Chicken Industry Key Facts 2021," accessed November 3, 2023, https://www.nationalchickencouncil.org/about-the-industry/statistics/broiler-chicken-industry-key-facts/.

16. Tom Polansek, "Insight: Bird Flu Spreads to New Countries, Threatens Non-Stop 'War' on Poultry," Reuters, March 15, 2023, https://www.reuters.com/world/bird-flu-spreads-new-countries-threatens-non-stop-war-poultry-2023-02-15/.

17. USDA, Foreign Agricultural Service, "African Swine Fever in Xingjiang Notified," Attaché Report CH2022-0027, March 3, 2022, https://www.fas.usda.gov/data/china-african-swine-fever-xinjiang-notified.

18. Alecia Larew et al., "Bovine Tuberculosis Eradication in the United States: A Century of Progress," in *Zoonotic Tuberculosis: Mycobacterium and Other Pathogenic Mycobacteria*, eds. Charles O. Thoen, James H. Steele, and John B. Kaneene (New York: John Wiley, 2014), chapter 21, https://doi.org/10.1002/9781118474310.ch21.

19. William D. McBride and Nigel Key, *U.S. Hog Production From 1992 to 2009: Technology, Restructuring, and Productivity Growth*, USDA, Economic Research Service, ERR-158, October 2013, https://www.ers.usda.gov/webdocs/publications/45148/40364_err158.pdf.

20. Michael C. Brumm, "Space Allocation Decisions for Nursery and Grow-Finish Facilities," USDA, National Institute of Food and Agriculture, August 28, 2019, https://swine.extension.org/space-allocation-decisions-for-nursery-and-grow-finish-facilities/.

21. Brumm, "Space Allocation Decisions."

22. Quoted in Jodi Henke, "The Definition of Free-Range Chickens," *Successful Farming*, March 8, 2021, https://www.agriculture.com/podcast/living-the-country-life-radio/the-definition-of-free-range-chickens#.

23. Bill Bullard, "Under Siege: The U.S. Live Cattle Industry," *South Dakota Law Review* 58 (2013): 560.

24. C. Robert Taylor, "Harvested Cattle, Slaughtered Markets.?" April 27, 2022, available at SSRN, http://dx.doi.org/10.2139/ssrn.4094924.

25. USDA, *Agricultural Statistics 2019*.

26. Hendrickson et al., *Food System*.

27. USDA, *Agricultural Statistics 2019*.

Normalize from Reality

1. Food and Agriculture Organization of the United Nations, International Fund for Agricultural Development, UNICEF, World Food Programme, and World Health Organization, *The State of Food Security and Nutrition in the World 2021* (Food and Agriculture Organization of the United States: Rome, 2021), https://www.fao.org/agrifood-economics/publications/detail/en/c/1201877/.

2. Lee Benson, "The World's Largest and Possibly Oldest Living Organism Lives in Utah," *Deseret News*, August 15, 2021, https://www.deseret.com/utah/2021/8/15/22609608/worlds-largest-and-possibly-oldest-living-organism-resides-in-utah-aspens.

3. "Public and Private Land Percentages by US States," SummitPost, accessed November 4, 2023, https://www.summitpost.org/public-and-private-land-percentages-by-us-states/186111.

4. Patrick Lohmann, "$1.45 Billion More Likely Coming to Victims of Hermits Peak–Calf Canyon Fire," *Source NM*, December 20, 2002, https://sourcenm.com/2022/12/20/1-45-billion-more-likely-coming-to-victims-of-hermits-peak-calf-canyon-fire/.

5. Robyn Boere and Neil Stange, letter to the editor, *Economist*, November 7, 2020.

6. Livestock Loss Board, *Livestock Loss Board 2020 Biennial Report*, a report to Legislative Economic Affairs Interim Committee, 2020, https://leg.mt.gov/content/Committees/Interim/2019-2020/Economic-Affairs/Meetings/Sept-2020/Livestock-loss-report2020.pdf.

7. Livestock Loss Board, *Livestock Loss Board 2020 Biennial Report*.

8. Livestock Loss Board, *Livestock Loss Board 2020 Biennial Report*.
9. National Park Service, Yellowstone, "Gray Wolf," https://www.nps.gov/yell/learn/nature/wolves.htm, last modified April 25, 2023.
10. National Park Service, Yellowstone, "Elk," https://www.nps.gov/yell/learn/nature/elk.htm, last modified October 26, 2023.
11. National Park Service, Yellowstone, "Moose," https://www.nps.gov/yell/learn/nature/moose.htm, last modified April 24, 2023.
12. National Park Service, Yellowstone, "Bison," https://www.nps.gov/yell/learn/nature/bison.htm, last modified April 25, 2023; National Park Service, Yellowstone, "Bison Management," https://www.nps.gov/yell/learn/management/bison-management.htm, last modified August 9, 2023.
13. For an example covering central Montana, see US Department of the Interior, BLM, *Lewistown Proposed Resource Management Plan and Final Environmental Impact Statement*, February 2020, https://eplanning.blm.gov/public_projects/lup/38214/20012601/250017167/Lewistown_PRMP_FEIS_Vol_1_Feb2020.pdf.
14. Mary Meagher and Margaret E. Meyer, "On the Origin of Brucellosis in Bison of Yellowstone National Park," *Conservation Biology* 8, no. 3 (September 1994): 645–53.
15. Wikipedia, "American bison," last modified October 20, 2023, 00:22, https://en.wikipedia.org/wiki/American_bison.
16. "Grizzly Bear Population by State," World Population Review, last modified March 2023, https://worldpopulationreview.com/state-rankings/grizzly-bear-population-by-state; Philip D. McLoughlin and Gordon B. Stenhouse, *Mapping Ecological Data and Status of Grizzly Bears (Ursus arctos) in Canada*, technical report to NatureServe Canada, May 1, 2021, https://www.natureserve.org/sites/default/files/2021-10/McLoughlin%20and%20Stenhouse%20%282021%29%20Grizzly%20Bear%20Mapping%20in%20Canada%20%28FINAL%20Report%2C%20May%201%20 2021%29_0.pdf.
17. National Park Service, Yellowstone, "Grizzly Bear," https://www.nps.gov/yell/learn/nature/grizzlybear.htm, last modified April 23, 2023.
18. Cecily M. Costello, Justin Dellinger, Jennifer K. Fortin-Noreus, Mark A. Haroldson, Wayne F. Kasworm, Lori L. Roberts, Justin E. Tiesberg, and Frank T. van Manen, *A Summary of Grizzly Bear Distribution in Montana: Application of consistent Methods in 2022*, United States Geographical Survey, 2023, https://fwp.mt.gov/binaries/content/assets/fwp/conservation/bears/a-summary-of-grizzly-bear-distribution-in-montana-2022_20230815.pdf; David Murray, "Change in Administration Won't Necessarily End Federal Efforts to Delist Grizzly Bears Protections," *Great Falls Tribune*,

November 30, 2020, https://www.greatfallstribune.com/story/news/2020/11/30/montana-grizzly-bear-population-grow-near-extinction/6432036002/.

19. Katie Hill, "Wildlife Advocates Sue Feds for Trapping, Relocating, and Killing Problem Grizzlies," OutdoorLife, January 23, 2023, https://www.outdoorlife.com/conservation/wildlife-advocates-sue-feds-for-trapping-relocating-and-killing-problem-grizzlies/.

The Complicity of Consumers

1. USDA, Economic Research Service, "Food Prices and Spending," last modified September 26, 2023, https://www.ers.usda.gov/data-products/ag-and-food-statistics-charting-the-essentials/food-prices-and-spending/.

2. USDA, "Food Prices and Spending."

3. "NFU: U.S. Farmers' Earnings from Food Dollar Hit Historic Low at Less Than 15 Cents; Less Than 5 Cents for Potato Chips," July 2, 2023, Potato News Today, https://www.potatonewstoday.com/2023/07/03/nfu-u-s-farmers-earnings-from-food-dollar-hit-historic-low-at-less-than-15-cents-less-than-5-cents-for-potato-chips/.

4. National Farmers Union, "The Farmer's Share," accessed November 4, 2023, https://nfu.org/farmers-share/.

5. USDA, *Agricultural Statistics 2019*.

6. United Food and Commercial Workers International Union, "Meatpacking Worker COVID Cases Triple Previous Estimates with At Least 59,000 Workers Infected Nationwide, Major Safety Failures in Non-Union Plants," press release, October 27, 2021, https://www.ufcw.org/press-releases/new-report-meatpacking-worker-covid-cases-triple-previous-estimates-with-at-least-59000-workers-infected-nationwide-major-safety-failures-in-non-union-plants/.

7. Chuck Abbott, "As Meat Plants Slow, U.S. Will Help Growers Kill Livestock," Successful Farming, April 27, 2020, https://www.agriculture.com/news/livestock/as-meat-plants-slow-us-will-help-growers-kill-livestock.

8. Donald J. Trump quoted in Katherine Faulders, "Trumps Signs Executive Order to Keep Meat Processing Plants Open under Defense Production Act," *ABC News*, April 28, 2020, https://abcnews.go.com/Politics/trump-sign-executive-order-meat-processing-plants-open/story?id=70389089.

9. Greg Henderson, "Profit Tracker: Growing Packer/Feeder Margin Spread,"

Farm Journal, AgWeb.com, February 3, 2021, https://www.agweb.com/markets/livestock-markets/profit-tracker-growing-packer/feeder-margin-spread.

10. Carey Gillam and Aliya Uteuova, "Popular Weedkiller Roundup on Trial Again as Cancer Victims Demand Justice," *Guardian*, August 23, 2022, https://www.theguardian.com/us-news/2022/aug/23/bayer-roundup-monsanto-epa-trial-cancer-victims.

11. Savory Institute, "Holistic Management," accessed October 20, 2023, https://savory.global/holistic-management/.

12. Allan Savory, *Holistic Management: A Commonsense Revolution to Restore our Environment*, 3rd ed. (Washington, DC: Island Press: 2017).

The Not COOL Story of the Farm Policy Debate

1. Recognizing the Duty of the Federal Government to Create a Green New Deal, H.R. 109, 116th Cong. (2019).

2. Joel L. Greene, *USDA's 'GIPSA Rule' on Livestock and Poultry Marketing Practice*, Congressional Research Service, updated January 7, 2016, https://crsreports.congress.gov/product/pdf/R/R41673.

3. Nancy Fink Huehnergarth, "Quashing Consumers' Right-To-Know, Congress Repeals Country-Of-Origin-Labeling for Beef and Pork," *Forbes Magazine*, December 12, 2015.

4. Huehnergarth, "Quashing Consumers' Right-To-Know."

5. Ross Hallren and Alexandra Opanasets, "Whence the Beef: The Effect of Repealing Mandatory Country of Origin Labeling (COOL) Using a Vertically Integrated Armington Model with Monte Carlo Simulation," *Southern Economic Journal* 84, no. 3 (January 2018), 879–97. https://doi.org/10.1002/soej.12248.

6. Exec. Order No. 14036, 86 Fed. Reg. 36987 (Executive Order on Promoting Competition in the American Economy) (2021).

7. For further information concerning the structure of livestock and underlying economic theory, see Francisco Garrido, Minji Kim, Nathan H. Miller, and Matthew C. Weinberg, "Buyer Power in the Beef Packing Industry: An Update on Research in Progress," Georgetown University, April 13, 2022, http://www.nathanhmiller.org/cattlemarkets.pdf; C. Robert Taylor, "Harvested Cattle, Slaughtered Markets?" (April 27, 2022), http://dx.doi.org/10.2139/ssrn.4094924; Christopher C. Pudenz and Lee L. Schulz, "Multi-plant Coordination in the US Beef Packing Industry," *American Journal of Agricultural Economics*, March 23, 2023, https://doi.org/10.1111/ajae.12391; Peter Carstensen, "Doctor Pangloss as an Agricultural Economist: The

Analytic Failures of the U.S. Beef Supply Chain: Issues and Challenges," *Univ. of Wisconsin Legal Studies*, research paper no. 1741, March 4, 2022, https://papers.ssrn.com/sol3/papers.cfm?abstract_id=4049230.

8. Garrido et al., "Buyer Power"; Taylor, "Harvested Cattle"; Pudenz and Schulz, "Multi-plant Coordination."

9. Cattle Price Discovery and Transparency Act of 2021, S. 3229, 117th Cong. (2021).

10. *Beefing up Competition: Examining America's Food Supply Chain: Hearing Before the U.S. Senate Committee on the Judiciary*, 117th Cong., July 28, 2021, https://www.judiciary.senate.gov/committee-activity/hearings/beefing-up-competition-examining-americas-food-supply-chain.

11. National Family Farm Coalition, *Milk from Family Dairies Act*, 2021, https://nffc.net/wp-content/uploads/Milk-from-Family-Dairies-Act-policy-detail.pdf.

12. Energy Independence and Security Act of 2007, Pub. L. No. 110-140, 121 Stat. 1492 (2007).

13. Bart L. Fisher, Joe L. Outlaw, and David P. Anderson, eds. *The U.S. Beef Supply Chain: Issues and Challenges* (College Station: Agriculture and Food Policy Center, Texas A&M University, 2021).

14. Sarah A. Low et al., *Trends in U.S. Local and Regional Food Systems: Report to Congress*, AP-068, USDA, Economic Research Service, January 2015, https://www.ers.usda.gov/webdocs/publications/42805/51173_ap068.pdf?v=6270.3.

15. Low et al., *Trends in U.S. Local and Regional Food Systems*.

16. Steve W. Martinez and Timothy Park, *Marketing Practices and Financial Performance of Local Food Producers: A Comparison of Beginning and Experienced Farmers*, USDA, Economic Research Service, EIB-225, August 2021, https://www.ers.usda.gov/publications/pub-details/?pubid=101785.

17. Proposing an Amendment to the Constitution of the United States Relating to Contributions and Expenditures Intended to Affect Elections, H.J.R. 2, 116th Cong. (2019).

18. Morning Consult, National Tracking Poll, September 14–16, 2022, https://www.r-calfusa.com/wp-content/uploads/2022/09/2209105_topline_COALITION_FOR_PROSPEROUS_AMERICA_RVs.pdf.

19. Sally J. Herrin, "Country of Origin Labeling and the Specious Logic of the NCBA," *North Platte Bulletin*, October 6, 2013.

20. Lauren Manning, "Should Imported Beef Carry a U.S.A. Label?," Sacred Cow, May 13, 2020, https://www.sacredcow.info/blog/country-of-origin-beef-labeling.

21. NAMI, "About NAMI," accessed November 4, 2023, https://www.meatinstitute.org/About_NAMI.

22. National Cattlemen's Beef Association website, accessed October 20, 2023, https://www.tsln.com/profile/national-cattlemens-beef-association/.

23. USDA, *Agricultural Statistics 2019*.

24. Beef Promotion and Research Act of 1985, Pub. L. 99-198, 99 Stat. 1597 (1985).

25. Anna McConnell, "SF Special: Constant Battle for Beef Checkoff Transparency," Successful Farming, March 21, 2017, https://www.agriculture.com/livestock/cattle/a-constant-battle-for-beef-checkoff-transparency.

26. American Farm Bureau Federation website, accessed October 20, 2023, https://www.fb.org.

27. National Farmers Union, "About NFU," accessed October 20, 2023, https://nfu.org/about/.

28. USDA, *Agricultural Statistics 2019*.

Bridging the Rural-Urban Divide

1. An Act Revising Laws Related to Local Boards of Health, H.B. 121, 67th Montana Leg, 2021.

2. An Act Generally Revising Gun Laws, H.B. 102, 67th Montana Legislature, 2021.

3. An Act Providing for a Youth Health Protection Act, S.B. 99, 68th Montana Legislature, 2023.

4. BLM, "BLM Issues Final Decision on Bison Grazing Proposal," press release, July 28, 2022, https://www.blm.gov/press-release/blm-issues-final-decision-bison-grazing-proposal.

5. "JBS: Cyber-Attack Hits World's Largest Meat Supplier, BBC, June 2, 2021, https://www.bbc.com/news/world-us-canada-57318965.

6. United Nations, "UN Climate Report: It's 'Now or Never' to Limit Global Warming to 1.5 Degrees," *UN News*, April 4, 2022, https://news.un.org/en/story/2022/04/1115452.

7. USDA, Economic Research Service, "Data Show U.S. Poverty Rates in 2019 Higher in Rural Areas Than in Urban for Racial/Ethnic Groups," chart, last updated August 23, 2021, https://www.ers.usda.gov/data-products/chart-gallery/gallery/chart-detail/?chartId=101903.

8. Daniel M. Hurley, "A Sequential Relationship: Drought's Contribution to the Onset of the Syrian Civil War," *Journal of International Relations*, December 12, 2018, http://www.sirjournal.org/research/2018/12/12/a-sequential-relationship-droughts-contribution-to-the-onset-of-the-syrian-civil-war.

INDEX

AFBF. *See* American Farm Bureau Federation
Africa: advice to, 55; grazing in, 98; rural-urban divide in, 2–3. *See also* Ethiopia; Kenya; Somalia
African swine fever (ASF), 35, 94
Against the Grain (Scott), 3–4
agriculture, xvii; agrotechnology in, 28–29, 46, 91–92; biodiversity and, 61–64; cities and, 3; classification in, 13; corporate farming in, 13–14; crop farming in, 115–17; dispiriting economics of, 12–14; drought impacting, 19; efficiency in, 21–22, 24; environmental movement and, 12–13, 56, 62–63; export and, 22–24, 30, 116; flexibility in, 46–47; get big or get out in, 19–21; globalization impacting, 94; during Great Depression, 19–20; historical perspective on, 90–94; land use of, 12, 86–87, 91; land value and, 13–14; market competition in, 43–44, 46, 63, 92, 113–15, 138–39; market reformation in, 49–53, 111–12; monoculture in, 49–50, 63–64, 93–94, 100; monopolies and neoliberalism in, 27–30; myths and half truths in, 95–96; neoliberalism or nouveau fascism in, 25–27; other initiatives for, 110–13; overproduction in, 20; plant fencerow to fencerow in, 21–24; policies against, xviii, 4, 24, 44, 55–56, 92; sectors requiring reform in, 115–17; slavery and, 1, 3; solutions for, 45–49, 101–3; subsidies in, 17–18, 24, 92; trade deficit and, 15; what to do about, 44–53; wildlife, recreation and, 71–74. *See also* farmers; food; industrialized agriculture; precision agriculture; ranching; small family farms
Albertsons, 42, 52
American Addiction Centers, 4
American Farm Bureau Federation (AFBF), 127–28
American Fur Company, x
American Prairie Reserve (APR), 69–70, 132
animal rights advocates, 58
antitrust laws, 43, 52, 112. *See also* Packers and Stockyards Act of 1921
APR. *See* American Prairie Reserve
Armour & Company, 108
ASF. *See* African swine fever
avian influenza, 34–35, 94

Bayer, 28, 93, 122
bears. *See* grizzly bears
Bear Wags Its Tail creek, ix. *See also* MacDonald Creek
beef: *vs.* fake meat, 47; labeling of, 36, 109–10, 123–24. *See also* cattle
Biden, Joseph, 105, 110–11, 113
biodiversity: agriculture and, 61–64; genetic traits in, 64; land management and, 62; monocultures *vs.*, 63–64

bison, xvii; APR for, 69–70, 132; brucellosis impacting, 78–79; wolves and, 75, 77, 78; in Yellowstone National Park, 78–80
BLM. *See* Bureau of Land Management
Boere, Robyn, 70
Booker, Cory, 106. *See also* Farm System Reform Act of 2021
Bork, Robert, 25–26
Borlaug, Norman, 24
bovine spongiform encephalopathy (BSE), 35
bovine tuberculosis, 35
brucellosis: bison impacted by, 78–79; transmission of, 79–80
Bryan, William Jennings, 85
BSE. *See* bovine spongiform encephalopathy
Buffalo Commons, xv–xvi, 132
Buffalo Field Campaign, 78–79
Bullard, Bill, 39–40
Bundy family protests, 72
Bunge Corporation, 29–30, 51
Bureau of Land Management (BLM), 12, 19
Butz, Earl, 21, 92
buy-local system. *See* local foods movement

CAFOs. *See* Concentrated Animal Feeding Operations
Canadian Cattle Association (CCA), 124–25
Cargill, 29–30
cartels: benefit of, 86; for cattle, 29–31, 51, 90, 112; for chickens, 29–34; in China, 28; for corn, 29–30; for dairy, 42; for farm equipment, 114; fertilizer and, 28–30; for meat packing, 89–90, 108, 110–12, 120–21; for meat proteins, 27–28; for pigs, 29–31, 36, 38, 51; in retail, 42–43; for seeds, 28–29; for soybeans, 29–30

cattle: bovine tuberculosis and, 35; BSE and, 35; cartels for, 29–31, 51, 90, 112; economics of, 87–88, 112; ethical questions about, 57–58; feed for, xvii–xviii, 49; in feedlots, 38–40; FMD and, 35–36; gas emissions from, 47; manure from, 42; in Montana, 79; raising of, 39–40; as traumatized, 5. *See also* ranching
CCA. *See* Canadian Cattle Association
chickens: avian influenza impacting, 34–35, 94; in CAFOs, 31–34, 48; cartels for, 29–34; ethical issues surrounding, 48; exploitation of, 34; as free range, 38; manure of, 33; markets for, 31; processing of, 32–33
China: ASF in, 35; cartels in, 28; dairies in, 41; export to, 9, 23–24
Citizens United v. Federal Election Commission, 26, 122–23
Clark, Robert, Jr., 55
Clark, William, x
Clayton Act, 27
cliff paintings, x
climate change: carbon sequestration and, 95–96; contingencies lacking for, 86, 94, 116–17, 122, 129; cultural and political dimensions of, 140–41; dairies and, 115; decision making during, 130–31; deniers of, 83; farm bill on, 117–18; fascism and, 136; as faster than predicted, 134–35; future uncertain with, 53; as global problem, 45–46, 50, 56, 137; greenhouse gases and, 47; rural-urban divide and, 103, 134–35; vegetarianism and, 60; weather patterns during, 44–45, 64, 93
Concentrated Animal Feeding Operations (CAFOs): chickens in, 31–34, 48; ethical issues surrounding, 47–48; moratorium on, 106–7; pigs in, 36–38
conservationists/environmentalists: on bison, 78–80; on coyotes and wolves,

74–78; on forests, 67–68; on grizzly bears, 80–82; issues of, 64–65, 102; on land use, 66–71; magical thinking vs. reality of, 82–84; on mineral extraction, 65–66; perspective of, 62, 73; on rewilding, 70; trouble with, 64–82; on wildlife, recreation, and agriculture, 71–74
Conservation Reserve Program, 118
contract farming: of chickens, 31–34; of crops, 115–17; as sharecropping, 32
COOL. See Country of Origin Labeling
corn: arguments about, 47, 49; cartels for, 29–30; economics of, 15–17, 59–60; ethanol from, 15, 59, 117; for livestock, 15, 47, 49; overproduction of, 45, 59–60, 92, 117–18; vulnerability of, 100
Corteva, 28
Country of Origin Labeling (COOL): opposition to, 124; "Product of USA" label and, 109–10; story of, 123–29; tribunal against, 124–35
COVID-19 pandemic: food chain during, 88–89; food cost during, 85, 121; food shortages during, 50; industrialized agriculture during, 9; meat packing during, 88–90, 112, 121, 133; Montana during, 131; rural America during, 132; subsidies during, 18; supply chains during, 88–89, 133
coyotes: livestock killed by, 84; wolves and, 74–78
crop insurance, 24
Crow (Apsáalooke), x
cultural landscape, 2

dairies: cartels for, 42; climate change impacting, 115; policy for, 41, 114–15; water and, 41–42
Dante Alighieri, 130
Darwin, Charles, 57–58

Defense Production Act, 90
Democracy for All Amendment, 123
Democratic Party, 134
Diamond, Jared, 7, 144n5
Dreyfus. See Louis Dreyfus Company

economic migration, 136–37. See also immigrant workers
elephants, 71–72
elk, 69, 77, 82–83
environmentalist. See conservationists/environmentalists
Erikson, Julia, xi–xii, 19
ethanol, 15, 59, 117
Ethiopia, 54
export: agriculture and, 22–24, 30, 116; to China, 9, 23–24; Yeutter for, 22

factory farms. See Concentrated Animal Feeding Operations
famine, 136
Farm Aid concerts, 46
farm bills: on climate change, 117–18; COOL in, 124; failures of, 23–24; Freedom to Farm Act, 24; future, 52, 117–18; in 1960s, 20–21; in 1980s, 23
farm equipment, 28, 114
farmers: anger of, 8–9; commodity selling by, 29–30; as conservative, 105; crop cost for, 15–16; economic reality of, 15–18, 87–88; generations in, 14, 18; in industrialized agriculture, 1–2; inputs for, 28–29; land cost for, 15, 17, 22; myth about, 2; negative income for, 16; products raised by, 14–15; respect lacking for, 11; substance abuse by, 4; as underprivileged, 46; against WOTUS, 106–7
farmers' markets: customer loyalty at, 121; organic products at, 87; supply for, 86
farmgate prices, 85–86
farming. See agriculture

Index | 155

Farm System Reform Act of 2021: captive supply reform under, 107–8; COOL and "Product of USA" label under, 109–10; GIPSA rules under, 108–9; moratorium on large CAFOs under, 106–7

fascism: Americans against, 136; climate change and, 136; definition of, 26; neoliberalism and, 25–27; Trump in, 26–27

fertilizer: Cargill and, 30; cartels and, 28–30; as input, 28–29; introduction of, 20, 91; precision ag and, 28, 122; regenerative farming and, 97

FMD. *See* foot-and-mouth disease

food: abundance of, 85; climate change impacting, 134–35; cost of, 85, 101, 129; during COVID-19, 88–89; direct-to-consumer markets for, 118–23; in France, 118–20; future of, 100–1, 103; historical perspective on, 90–94; price and, 120–21; respect lacking for, 10–11; significance of, 139–40; world market for, 116–17

Food and Agriculture Act of 1965, 21

food insecurity, 59

foot-and-mouth disease (FMD), 35–36

France: Les Halles in, 118–19; Marchés d'Intérêt National law in, 120

Freedom to Farm Act, 24

free range, 38

Friedman, Milton, 25–26

fur, 74

genetically modified organism (GMO), 28, 93–94

Gianforte, Greg, 133

GIPSA. *See* Grain Inspection Packers and Stockyards Administration

Glacier National Park: adjoining wilderness area to, 81; grizzly bears in, 80–82; interbreeding in, 81–82; tourists in, 80

globalization, 94

global warming. *See* climate change

glyphosate, 94

GMO. *See* genetically modified organism

gold mining, x

Grain Inspection Packers and Stockyards Administration (GIPSA): Farm System Reform Act of 2021 and, 108–9; Promoting Competition in the American Economy and, 114; Trump against, 109, 114

Grassley, Chuck, 111–12

Grass Range, xi–xii; abandoning of, xiii–xiv; development of, xiii; retirees in, xiv

Grass Range High School, xiii–xiv

Grass Range History Committee, xiii

grazing: in Africa, 98; in Montana, 79–80, 99

Green New Deal, 53, 105–6

grizzly bears: conservationists on, 80–82; as dangerous, 81, 131–32; interbreeding of, 82; in Montana, 72, 81; in national parks, 80–82; numbers of, 80–81; politics and, 83

guns, x; god, walls and, 5–8; Montana laws for, 131

Les Halles, 118–19

Hermes, Jim, 38

Herrin, Sally J., 124

hobby farmers, 20

hogs. *See* pigs

Holistic Resource Management (HRM), 98–99

homesteading, xi; railroad and, xiii; ranching and, xvi; remains of, 19; revisionist history of, xii

HRM. *See* Holistic Resource Management

hunter-gatherers, 3, 58

hunting reserve, 69

IBMP. *See* Interagency Bison Management Plan
immigrant workers, 5; chicken processing by, 33; Trump against, 26–27
industrialized agriculture: beginning of, 1; during COVID-19, 9; farmers lacking in, 1–2; industrial agribusiness and, 88–90; respect lacking in, 10–11
Interagency Bison Management Plan (IBMP), 79–80
Iowa: climate change impacting, 44; corn produced in, 49; economic realities in, 15–17; surplus from, 59–60

JBS Foods: as cattle cartel, 29, 31, 90, 112; as chicken cartel, 29, 31; during COVID-19, 90, 112; in meat protein production, 31, 36; as pork cartel, 29, 31, 36; Russian cyber attack on, 133
The Jungle (Sinclair), 108

Kenya, 72
Kittelson, Anna, xii
Kroger, 42, 52

land-grant universities, 91, 122
landscape, 2
landscape ecology, 2
Lewis, Meriwether, x
local foods movement, 32, 38. *See also* farmers' markets
logging, 68
Lorenzi, Henry, 55
Louis Dreyfus Company, 29–30, 51
Lynn, Barry, 25–26

MacDonald, Henry: as namesake, ix; Sioux and, x–xi; as trapper, x
MacDonald Creek, ix
mad cow disease. *See* bovine spongiform encephalopathy
mandatory market reporting, 111
Matthews, Anne, xv–xvi

meat packing: cartels for, 89–90, 108, 110–12, 120–21; chickens in, 32–33; during COVID-19, 88–90, 112, 121, 133; Trump, workers and, 89–90
Mesopotamia, 3
migrant workers. *See* immigrant workers
Milk from Family Dairies Act, 114–15
mineral extraction, x, 65–66, 73
mining. *See* mineral extraction
monopolies: commodity selling in, 29–30; illusion under, 100–1; inputs in, 28–29; meat protein cartel in, 27–28; neoliberalism and, 27–30. *See also* cartel
Monsanto, 28, 93–94, 96
Montana: bison in, 78–79; cattle in, 79; cliff paintings in, x, 143n1; climate of, 19, 79; during COVID-19, 131; crop fields in, 96; grasslands in, xvi; grazing in, 79–80, 99; grizzly bears in, 72, 81; gun laws in, 131; land use in, 66–67, 73; livestock in, xi; mining in, x, 65–66, 73; politics in, 83, 134; Sioux raids in, xi; ultrawealthy landowners in, xviii, 132–33; wolves in, 75–76
moose, 78

NAFTA. *See* North American Free Trade Agreement
NAMI. *See* North American Meat Institute
National Cattlemen's Beef Association (NCBA), 124, 126–27
National Chicken Council, 34
National Farmers Union (NFU), 127–28
NCBA. *See* National Cattlemen's Beef Association
neoliberalism: in agriculture, 25–27, 51; dairy farms and, 41; definition of, 25; failure of, 27, 90, 138; internal logic of, 88; monopolies and, 27–30
NFU. *See* National Farmers Union

Index | 157

North American Free Trade Agreement (NAFTA), 35, 123
North American Meat Institute (NAMI), 124–25

Ocasio-Cortez, Alexandria, 53, 105
Ogallala Aquifer, 118
organic farming, 86–87

Packers and Stockyards Act of 1921 (P&S Act): GIPSA rules and, 108–9; ignoring of, 27; *The Jungle* influencing, 108; for livestock producers, 116; as precedent, 50–51; strength of, 107
parity, 16
pigs: ASF and, 35; in CAFOs, 36–38; cartels for, 29–31, 36, 38, 51; during COVID-19, 89; labeling of, 36, 109–10; porcine epidemic diarrhea virus and, 35; raising of, 36–37
Plains Indians, x, 143n1
plowing, 94–95
political extremist personality disorder, 5–6
Popper, Deborah, xv–xvi, xviii, 132
Popper, Frank, xv–xvi, xviii, 132
porcine epidemic diarrhea virus, 35
pork. *See* pigs
prairie, 69–70, 118. *See also* American Prairie Reserve
precision agriculture, 28–29, 122
prescribed burns, 68
price discovery, 43
"Product of USA" label, 36; COOL and, 109–10; Promoting Competition in the American Economy on, 113
Promoting Competition in the American Economy: dairies omitted in, 114–15; on GIPSA rules, 114; on "Product of USA" label, 113; on right to repair, 114
P&S Act. *See* Packers and Stockyards Act of 1921

Ranchers-Cattlemen Action Legal Fund United Stockgrowers of America, 128
ranching: anger in, 8–9; economics of, 87–88; grass for, xvii–xviii; homesteading and, xvi; water and, xvi–xvii
Ray, Daryll, 23
Reagan, Ronald, 21, 26
regenerative farming: myths and half truths about, 95–96; prairie and, 118; road map lacking for, 97–98. *See also* Holistic Resource Management
Republican Party: in Montana, 83; NCBA and, 126; rural votes for, 4–5; wolves and, 83; Yeutter in, 21. *See also* Trump, Donald
retail: cartels in, 42–43; deregulation and, 138; restoration of, 52
rewilding, 70
right to repair, 114
Rosendale, Matt, 133
Roundup, 93–94, 96
rural America: anger in, 8–9; class society in, 4–5; during COVID-19, 132; decline of, 9, 92; farm bills impacting, 20–21; fear in, 7–8, 144n5; financial crisis impacting, 22–23; guns, god, and walls in, 5–8; as pro-life, 6; Republican votes by, 4–5; revitalization of, 52–53; substance abuse in, 4–5; technology and, 6–7
rural-urban divide, 53; bridge building in, 139–41; climate change and, 103, 134–35; Dante's sheep and, 135–39; environmentalism in, 73–74; fluidity in, 3–4; as global, 2–3; land use and, 12–13; magical thinking *vs.* reality in, 82–84; political dysfunction in, 136; political environment impacting, 131; power disparity in, 140
Russia, 90–91

Sanders, Bernie, 106
Savory, Allan, 98–99

Schaffer, Harwood, 23
Scott, James C., 3–4
Second Amendment, 6, 139
seeds, 28–29
Sherman Antitrust Act, 27
Sinclair, Upton, 108
Sioux: in intertribal wars, x; raids by, xi
slavery, 1, 3
small family farms, 14; assets and, 16–17; off-farm income for, 17, 135; sales by, 2, 13; subsidies for, 17–18
soil carbon sequestration. *See* regenerative farming
soil fertility, xii, 62
Somalia, 54
sorghum, 54
Soviet Union, 90–91
soybeans, 15; arguments about, 49; cartels for, 29–30; overproduction of, 45, 59
spot market, 111, 113
Stange, Neil, 70
Steinbeck, John, 10, 20
Stockton, Bill, ix, xiii
Stockton, William Murray, Sr., xi–xii, 19
subsidies, 17–18, 24
substance abuse, 4–5
sustainable agriculture, xvi
Swift & Company, 108
swine flu, 94
Syngenta, 28, 122
Syria, 136–37

taxes, 26
Tester, Jon, 111
Trump, Donald: empty promises of, 105; as fascist, 26–27; against GIPSA rules, 109, 114; against immigrant workers, 26–27; against packing plant workers, 89–90; regulations reversed by, 114
Tyson Fresh Meats: CAFOs pioneered by, 31–32; as cattle cartel, 29, 31; as chicken cartel, 29, 31–34; contract farming and, 31–32; during COVID-19, 89–90, 112; efficiency of, 32–33; exploitation by, 34; immigrant workers for, 33; as pork cartel, 29, 31, 36; Trump and, 89

United States Cattlemen's Association, 128
US Fish and Wildlife Service, 81–82

vegetarians: environmental reasons for, 58–60; ethical reasons for, 56–57; meat-substitutes for, 47; nonsolution of, 56–60
Volcker, Paul, 26

Walmart, 42, 52, 100
Warren, Elizabeth, 106
water: dairies and, 41–42; ranching and, xvi–xvii
Waters of the United States (WOTUS), 106–7
Western Organization of Resource Councils, 108
wildfires, 67–68, 130
wolves: bison and, 75, 77, 78; coyotes and, 74–78; dangers of, 75, 102; elk and, 77; losses from, 75–76; Republican politicians and, 83; in Yellowstone National Park, 74–75, 77, 82, 102
World War II, 20, 59, 85, 91
WOTUS. *See* Waters of the United States

Yellowstone National Park: bison in, 78–80; elk in, 82–83; grizzly bears in, 80–82; moose in, 78; overgrazing in, 79–80; wolves in, 74–75, 77, 82
Yeutter, Clayton: for export, 22; regulations reduced by, 26; as Republican, 21

www.ingramcontent.com/pod-product-compliance
Lightning Source LLC
Chambersburg PA
CBHW030104170825
30846CB00002B/25